Light On the Dark Side of God

Second Edition
by M. M. Campbell

Dedicated to

God's invisible church on earth

ISBN 0-9741841-0-1

Edited by Janice Longpre
Cover design by Ed Guthero
Cover art by Darrel Tank

PRINTED IN USA

Published by:
Truth For the Final Generation
P. O. Box 216
Caldwell, Idaho 83605

TABLE OF CONTENTS

The anger of the Lord will not turn back until He has executed and performed the thoughts of His heart.
In the latter days you will understand it perfectly."
Jeremiah 23:20; 30:23,24.

INTRODUCTION

We have all seen optical illusions. A familiar one looks like a picture of a vase, to some people. But others see in the dark background instead, two profiles facing each other in silhouette.

Behold God taking vengeance on Sodom and Gomorrah, the people of Noah's time, lost souls of all the ages—and compare it with the compassionate character of Jesus Christ, who refused to hurt His enemies. They should match, according to Scripture. But do they? Is it possible we are looking at an optical illusion?

In recent years a number of believers have had a growing suspicion that Christianity itself has, in fact, embraced an illusion regarding the character of God—in particular the side having to do with His justice. These students of Scripture have explored some of the questions inherent in the traditional picture of a destroying God, with the result that a whole new picture of what constitutes His "wrath" is now emerging, fully harmonious with the gentle character of Christ. That new view is the subject of this work.

Christianity, deeply rooted in Judaism and for two thousand years anticipating Christ's return in glory, has a growing credibility problem that deepens with each passing century. Besides Christ's failure thus far to fulfill His promise to return, other factors combine to raise questions about Christianity's ability to survive into the coming years as a viable philosophy for thoughtful men and women. Some say God is dead; science in general concludes it has defeated Biblical perspectives; the gap widens between conservatives (generally Bible-believers) and liberals (generally not). Some have even declared our times "the post-Christian era."

How like God to let matters go almost to the point of hopelessness and then (to borrow from the language of gaming) to play His final trump card and take the whole pot, as a surprised world looks on.

Who needs this book? Thinking men and women everywhere, especially those who have given Christianity "a pass" because they have observed the very problems in Christian thought this book addresses. If you reject a God who burns the lost unendingly, this book is for you. If you have come to Christ as the Being who invented total other-centered love (perhaps in spite of the puzzle of His, in the end, burning people), then this work will bring you enormous relief. If you are one who has never understood how the gospel works, this book is for you.

A Savior Across the Boundaries

God has seen fit to connect the history of truth with the history of Israel. It is therefore impossible to examine Biblical truth and ignore this ancient people, particularly when Scripture holds them up as an example for our times (1 Corinthians 10:11). Given our vital modern concern for tolerance, I hesitate to depict Israel in less than flattering terms and would never do so, except for the very plain statements of Scripture.

We will agree, I am certain, that ancient Israel's history pertains not to that nation alone but to Christianity as well. Whatever is said of her is part of our own spiritual heritage. Nothing within this work should be construed as anything but an effort to take the history left for us in Scripture and to use it for its intended purpose of providing eternal, spiritual lessons. Christ came to "break down the middle wall of division between us, having abolished in His flesh the enmity . . . so as to create in Himself one new man from the two, thus making peace (Ephesians 2:14). The truth of God levels out the playing field for all humans; He is an equal opportunity Savior.

No effort has been made to establish that Jesus was, in fact, the God of the Old Testament (See 1 Corinthians 10:1; John 8:58), a position far more believable now than in the past in light of this new picture of God. It is important to understand that Jesus, the Old Testament God who taught Israel, could not always instruct them as he would ideally have liked, due to their slowness of heart [See, for example, Ezekiel 20:25, 26 (KJV); Matthew 5:21, 22, 27, 28, 33-37], *thus distorting our perceptions of Deity.* After completing this book, readers should see a new harmony between the character of the great "I Am," as the Old Testament presents Him, and that of Christ, as the gospels present Him—a harmony in favor of the compassionate character of our Lord Jesus Christ.

Mysteries Solved!

This new view of God illuminates many questions that have puzzled the world through the centuries, including the mystery of human suffering. As long as we are on this earth the righteous will have their moments of suffering, as did Job and Jesus, John the Baptist and the martyrs through the ages. We cannot necessarily know the reasons for the suffering of others, but in light of this new understanding of God we can often know the "why's" of our own suffering.

Does it follow the rule that we get the master we choose to obey? Does it follow the exception that proves the rule, which I call "The Job Syndrome"? Or are we looking at other knowable principles manifesting in adversity?

Other works have been and will continue to be published on this topic. Interested Bible students will want to consider the broad range of thinking from various sources regarding God's character, since all commentators do not see the matter (much less say it) exactly alike. However, may I at this point interject a personal note of caution regarding the efforts of some to take this new view of God in the direction of universalism—a direction in which I and many other responsible supporters of the view affirm it clearly does not go.

A Range of Gospel Topics

This work covers a lot of ground. While Christian writers have tended to focus one work on a single spiritual theme; such as prayer, faith, death, science and the Bible, that is not true of this work. It takes a number of pillars to uphold the picture of God's character of love. Therefore, in order to present this new perspective, it has been necessary to discuss, briefly, a wide range of interlocking gospel subjects that culminate in the revelation of God. A more complete presentation of each of these subjects appears in other works.

The Vindication of God

Somewhere, in the far reaches of the past, God's intelligent creation knew the truth about His character of love. But when it became in the interest of His enemy to distort that truth and thus to alienate their affections and their trust from Him, lies were told—lies that rolled on through the ages and became more venerated as they gathered age. But now it may be that God is placing a period at the end of the sentence with a picture of Himself more wonderful than we ever dared to dream.

May God guide you, as you consider Him in a beautiful new way. "Prove all things; hold fast that which is good" (1 Thessalonians 5:21).

OUR MISUNDERSTOOD GOD

*"The earth shall be full of
the knowledge of the Lord
as the waters cover the sea" (Isaiah 11:9).*

Years ago a realtor showed me a house as a possible purchase. It was a "fixer-upper," modestly priced, boasting a glorious eastern view from the large living room window. Rich dark grass and the thick hanging foliage of shade trees and ornamental bushes stretched out toward a patchwork valley floor, which faded into blue hills far in the distance. The view was everything the realtor said, from that direction. But he didn't say much about the back yard, set up against a rail fence that surrounded the local stockyards. Only a salesman could evaluate that house without reference to the back yard. When my thoughts turn to the Being we call "God," I often think of that house, for there is a wondrously strange side to our traditional view of God—a side that seems dark to us at times—a perplexing side scarcely mentioned from the pulpit today, even though it has puzzled thoughtful men and women for centuries, perhaps millennia.

"Sinners In the Hands of an Angry God"

In colonial America a Massachusetts minister named Jonathan Edwards, appalled at the worldliness creeping into his church, warned his parishioners of this "dark side" of God and the fate awaiting them if they continued in their unrepentant ways. No one since has described it better than he in his historic sermon, "Sinners in the Hands of an Angry God."

> The God that holds you over the pit of hell, much as one holds a spider, or some loathsome insect, over the fire, abhors you, and is dreadfully provoked; his wrath towards you burns like fire; he looks upon you as worthy of nothing else, but to be cast into the fire; he is of purer eyes than to bear to have you in his sight; you are ten thousand times more abominable in his eyes, as the most hateful and venomous serpent is in ours. You have offended him infinitely more than ever a stubborn rebel did his prince: and yet it is nothing but his hand that holds you from falling into the fire every moment: it is ascribed to nothing else, that

you did not go to hell the last night; that you was [sic] suffered to awake again in this world, after you closed your eyes to sleep; and there is no other reason to be given, why you have not dropped into hell since you arose in the morning, but that God's hand has held you up: there is no other reason to be given why you have not gone to hell, since you have sat here in the house of God, provoking his pure eyes by your sinful wicked manner of attending his solemn worship: yea, there is nothing else that is to be given as a reason why you do not at this very moment drop down into hell.

Edwards so moved his congregation with his view of God's character and the tortures of the damned, he sparked a revival known to history as the Great Awakening. Such is the power of a sermon well prepared. But his style has gone out of fashion among the clergy, and they, like my real estate salesman, generally consider it inappropriate to mention "the back yard" any more.

Ethical Problems

Despite the seemingly clear way in which Scripture presents Him, the traditional view of Christianity's God is heavy with ethical problems that have puzzled thoughtful men and women from time immemorial. As long as humans have reasoned on the subject of God, they have wondered about His destructive side. Noah's flood, Sodom and Gomorrah, eternal hell fire. . . . How can a God who punishes so cruelly also say: "I have no pleasure in the death of the wicked, but that the wicked turn from his way and live. Turn, turn from your evil ways! For why should you die?" "How can I give you up, Ephraim? How can I hand you over, Israel? . . . My heart churns within Me; My sympathy is stirred." "My heart sobs like a flute for Moab, sobs like a flute for the men of Kirheres; that accumulated treasure all lost" (Ezekiel 33: 11; Hosea 11:8; Jeremiah 48:36, JB). Would not humans manifesting this personality split be considered psychotic?

How can God exercise such "cruel and unusual" punishment as drowning the world, burning cities and the humans in them, and still be considered loving and just, as He and His adherents claim? He extended Himself to the lengths of Calvary to preserve our freedom of choice. But is choice really free, with God standing over us to destroy us if we choose wrong? After enduring the cross to redeem humanity, thus showing His loving character before the universe, why does He, in the end, reverse it all by executing those whose choices He does not like?

How can a God who kills command His people not to kill—and yet to be like Him in character? How does the mild and gentle Jesus reflect the character of the "fire-breathing" Old Testament God He came to reveal?

Perhaps nothing has contributed more to the advancement of atheism than these perplexing unanswered questions of Christianity.

The 19th century skeptic, Robert G. Ingersoll, spoke for multitudes through the ages, when he addressed the idea of an eternally burning hell in these words:"Infinite punishment is infinite cruelty, endless injustice, immortal meanness. . . .

"Christians have placed upon the throne of the universe a God of eternal hate. I cannot worship a being whose vengeance is boundless, whose cruelty shoreless, and whose malice is increased by the agonies he inflicts."[1] Those who believe hell eventually burns out still have the problem that an all-wise God, who is more loving than any human, could think of no better way to dispose of sin than to burn sinners, even though they are His children still—the creation of His own hand. If burning humans alive is inherently evil, then would it not be as evil an act for God as for humans? And God, as Christianity wishes to present Him, is not evil. Yet, evil is evil because it is evil. God's alleged participation in it does not sanctify it. The idea of hell fire, to many, constitutes another puzzling piece in Christianity's picture of God.

Is There Any Word From the Lord?

The past 100 years have seen almost miraculous advances in knowledge (see Daniel 12:4). Such fields of science as medicine and technology have introduced amazing innovations, many now several generations deep. But until recently that growth in knowledge has not extended to a heightened understanding of the word of God. Christianity has slumbered along, content with its own generally unchallenged orthodoxy. But as the world enters the 21st century, God's invisible church has reason to gaze heavenward and ask, "Is there any word from the Lord?" (Jeremiah 37:17).

The questions posed above have weighed down God's church from eons of ages past. As archeology slowly but steadily confirms Bible history, should we not also see an increase in our knowledge of the God of the Bible? Should not these questions find answers within the word itself, through the determined, prayerful efforts of Biblical scholars?

> Thus says the Lord:
>> "Let not the wise man glory in his wisdom,
>>> Let not the mighty man glory in his might,
>>>> Nor let the rich man glory in his riches;
>> But let him who glories glory in this,

---

[1] "The Great Infidels," 1881.

> *That he understands and knows Me,*[2]
> That I am the Lord, exercising,
> Lovingkindness, judgment, and
> righteousness in the earth.
> For in these I delight."   (Jeremiah 9:23, 24)

Our Misunderstood God

Some humans tremble to question God; they claim the Bible picture is too clear to doubt, that God punishes because He must. Only as the hand of God personally strikes, they say, can harmony reign in the social order. Who wants to live in a world overrun with crime and evil, where no barriers of coming judgment impede sin's onward march? Without question, Scripture speaks of judgment. "The wages of sin is death" (Romans 6:23), and nowhere in the pages of this work will you read otherwise.

But just as clearly, a close view of Scripture reveals God, in essence, crying out to be known and understood. If the surface view is all-sufficient, why would He plead, "Behold Me, behold Me" (Isaiah 65:1)? Why would He direct His people to "Lift up your voice with strength/Lift it up, be not afraid/Say to the cities of Judah/Behold your God!" (Isaiah 40:9).

A terrible situation existed in ancient Israel in the time of the prophets. The writings of the contemporaries Hosea, Isaiah, Amos and Micah, reflect the religious intensity of the times,[3] yet God declared through Hosea, "The Lord brings a charge against the inhabitants of the land: 'There is no truth or mercy or *knowledge of God* in the land" (4:1). The people were "destroyed for lack" of it (4:6). With all their religious fervor, they failed to pursue an accurate understanding of the God they claimed to worship, and their ignorance unfolded into wholesale sin and consequent vulnerability to surrounding nations. There is something about accuracy in our knowledge of God that brings right-doing, protection, power and blessings. This is not God's arbitrary decree, as we shall see; rather, it is a fail-safe default built into the realities of daily living on this planet.

We see ancient Israel's failure so clearly, but could we have the same need today and not see it? Might our own picture of God be suspect? Every element of our theology—our religious belief system—ultimately expresses how we see God. Life after death, the rapture/second coming, prophecy, eternal reward and punishment, the meaning of faith—the list goes on and on.

Try this exercise: List the various points of your religious belief system and analyze them in terms of what they say about God. Do you find Him reasonable? If we find ourselves asking, Why would He do that? Why would

---

[2]Italics are mine throughout, unless otherwise indicated.

[3]See Hosea 4:13; Isaiah 1:10-17; Amos 5:21-24; Micah 6:6-8.

He think that way, perhaps our view of God is faulty. In actual fact, God is consummately reasonable, as Bible prophets present Him, and He pleads for humans to relate to Him at that level (Isaiah 1:18). In its frequent Scriptural admonitions to study God, heaven is trying to tell us something. Let's not be too hasty to conclude we already understand.

The New Testament asserts perhaps even more strongly our need to pursue a better understanding of our Creator. God has given us powerful weapons to enhance our spiritual journey. In a text familiar to most Christians is a relevant and illuminating phrase. "The weapons of our warfare are not carnal, but mighty through God to the pulling down of strong holds; casting down imaginations and every high thing that exalteth itself against the *knowledge of God*" (2 Corinthians 10: 4,5, KJV). What do our spiritual weapons cast down? Strongholds. Imaginations. High things. All things, in fact that interfere with a true knowledge of God. Does this text say that an accurate knowledge of God is among the last things His enemy would have us know? Perhaps we should ask ourselves why.

Ephesians 4:13 predicts a time when God's invisible church will come together "in unity of the faith and *the knowledge of the Son of God*. Does this hint of a misunderstanding regarding the character of Deity, a misunderstanding soon to be clarified?

Isaiah 5:12 and 13 speaks of humans who "do not regard the work of the Lord, nor consider the operation of His hands [they don't understand Him?]. Therefore my people have gone into captivity, because they have no *knowledge*" [of God's character and purposes?]. Hebrews says, God's chosen "always go astray in their heart, and *they have not known My ways*" (3:10,11). This thought occurs over and over in Scripture.

"Come now, and let us reason together, says the Lord"; "Let us pursue *the knowledge of the Lord*" (Isaiah 1:18; Hosea 6:3). He invites discussion. He wants humans to take Him seriously and is willing to meet with us at any point of confusion, placing on record that He will not reject our sincere questions.

"This is eternal life," Jesus prayed, "that they may know You [God the Father], the only true God, and Jesus Christ whom You have sent" (John 17:3). Do we truly know God, as it is our privilege to know Him? As, in fact, we must know Him, if we would enter into life?

For when sin fades into history at last, God's people "shall not hurt nor destroy" in the kingdom made new. Why? "For the earth shall be full of *the knowledge of the Lord* as the waters cover the sea" (Isaiah 11:9,).

I have counted no less than 23 Biblical entries specifically directing us to come to a "knowledge" of God, and likely many more exist. Scripture is clear; we have misunderstood God; He desires to be known and has instructed us to make His character our study.

God's Character In His People

It was so important to God to be accurately understood that He sent His own Son into this world to reveal Him. We usually think of Christ as coming to save humans by offering Himself as a ransom for sin. While that is true, it is equally important and sometimes overlooked that He also came to reveal His Father's character to a fallen human race (John 10:30; 12:45:14:9; Hebrews 1:3; 2 Corinthians 4:6), thus underscoring Scripture's emphasis on the need of humans to know God accurately. Why would that need exist, if the world already understood?

The majority rejected Him, largely because they did not recognize His Father in Him. They wanted a replica of their view of the Old Testament God of war, who would free the nation from its humiliating bondage to the empire of Rome. What they got was an invitation to a Kingdom that dwelt in a converted heart, an opportunity to be better people, and the Judeo-Christian tradition has not yet reconciled the contrast between God as the Old Testament presents Him and as Christ presents Him in the New. Thus Christ was vilified and crucified as an imposter. Do we not deal with the same questions today regarding the contrast in character between Jesus and the sometimes brutal Old Testament God He came to reveal? Would we recognize our Lord today?

Transformation

Scripture further says God intends to reproduce His character in humans who agree to be so molded. Yet that transformation cannot take place where humans have any uncertainties or misunderstandings as to what constitutes God's character. Whether we acknowledge it or not, we are shaped largely by our belief regarding God. In fact, that may be the single most powerful factor in making us who we are. From the atheist or agnostic who gives free rein to sin, because he has no hope beyond this life, to one who becomes a model citizen because he recognizes that even a godless quasi-righteousness exalts a nation. From the religionist who refuses to carry arms in times of war to the genocidal maniac serving his concept of truth by stamping out God's "enemies." From everyday people going about the business of life to committed Christians pursuing a better understanding of the will of God, we are shaped to a greater or lesser degree by our thoughts regarding God and eternity. And humans who are so shaped shape the world. Without an accurate understanding of who God is, humanity serves a false god. Without an accurate understanding of God's character, human character declines, and the world reflects the loss.

Given our traditional view of God, Christians (like their concept of Him) are gentle and kind much of the time, except when the situation seems to call for gossip or destructive criticism or indifference to human woe or venting destructive emotions or taking human life. Isn't this how we see God's ways?

The human mind has an extraordinary capacity for kindness, except toward those "demonized" humans we believe God abhors. If we cause those to suffer, it's okay, we think. Doesn't God do the same?

Historically, the "church" has carried the traditional view of God to its logical conclusion by itself burning the opposition. Religious bigots have bloodied the pages of history with unspeakable crimes, which surely flowed out of their picture of God.[4]

Jesus predicted two thousand years ago that thus it would be. "The time is coming that whosoever kills you will think that he offers God service," He said (John 16:2). History confirms His prophecy. How could we, as Christians, have been so blind, so callous, so indifferent to human life? Jesus distills the answer down to its core. "These things they will do to you," He continues, "because they have not known the Father nor Me" (v. 3). Because Scripture gives so many examples of God's wiping out His enemies, Christians have become confused regarding the interpretation of Jesus' words. They have concluded that when we destroy them, we're doing so as God's agents, but when they destroy us, they are fulfilling this prediction. We see our enemy as God's enemy and ourselves as His sword of justice, because for war to occur in the first place the warriors must be made to see their cause as righteous and the enemy's as evil. Yet is it not possible that Jesus meant that wherever people kill each other in the name of religion, neither side bears the signet of the true and living God?

It takes little imagination to see that the traditional view of God as One who can reach a point where He employs deadly force could lead to deplorable conditions—where political power could be seen as a divine mandate to force the conscience of the politically weak. In czarist Russia, as well as pre-revolutionary France, for example, the church's connection with civil power engendered terrible abuses, causing an over-correction, which ended in atheistic regimes. Communism itself began as a protest against religious cruelty.

The Holocaust is a modern case in point, where a strong tradition of Judeo-Christian ethics didn't stop good and civilized people from supporting a regime which derived its power from the spilled blood of the governed and which attempted to exterminate an entire race perceived as undeserving of mercy. Where was the outrage, the conviction that causing the death of humans is intrinsically wrong?

---

[4]Henry Charles Lea, *A History of the Inquisition of the Middle Ages*. (New York: Harper & Brothers, Franklin Square, 1887), I, 222-3.

Northern Ireland, the Middle East, Bosnia, Kosovo further illustrate the passion with which each side, believing it carries the flag of God in a righteous cause, kills and maims innocent civilians and destroys its own homeland in a seemingly endless bloodletting, presumably praying for the blessing of its fierce, nationalistic God before sallying forth on missions of destruction. There are no wars bloodier than religious wars. Efforts to bring stability to such regions find religious fervor an almost impossible hurdle to overcome, politically generated peace accords notwithstanding.

And who can say if our traditional view of God as a destroyer has not in many ways encouraged the widespread secularization of our world, as thoughtful men and women see all this and note its inconsistency with mercy and justice—hallmark attributes of the Christian God of whom they have been told. History offers innumerable illustrations of the subtle and pernicious effects the traditional view of a destroying God has had on civilization. It has opened the door to injustice and persecution throughout time; paved the way for intolerance, bigotry and the imposing of religious laws and duties upon an unconvinced people. If God can use force to get attention, the logic runs, then believers may use similar tactics to do his work. Civilizations do not rise higher morally than their concept of Deity. "Ye are of your father . . . ," said Jesus, "and the works of your father ye will do" (John 8:44, KJV).

And history confirms it. Without a settled conviction that hurting and destroying others is inherently wrong, society positions itself over an ethical bottomless pit, with no protective absolutes to break its moral fall. Where shall we find a model for such settled conviction, if we cannot find it in God?

Coming To God

But aside from the profound affect our view of God has upon character, both individual and national, for the Christian, other compelling reasons exist to study God.

The quality of our prayer life, for example, depends largely upon the concept of God we bring to our communion with Him. If we believe His justice never preempts His love, with what confidence we may come before Him! From our prayer closet we emerge prepared to enter into all of life's experiences, assured that nothing can happen over which the God of love does not exercise absolute control. How easy we find it then to praise Him in all things, knowing "all things work together" for our good, because God really is Love, after all.

And, finally, there is this from the apostle John. "Beloved, now are we children of God, and it has not yet been revealed what we shall be, but we know that when He is revealed, we shall be like Him, for we shall see Him as

He is. And everyone who has this hope in Him purifies himself, just as He is pure" (1 John 3:2,3). And this purity, the character transformation enjoined in Scripture, occurs only as the result of knowing and loving a God who is Himself love personified and therefore worthy of our love and imitation. Calvary argues eloquently in favor of His being such a God, but what do we do with that Biblical eternal fire?

While both history and surface Scripture represent God as a destroyer, the nagging questions suggest there is more to understand. Could He be talking "apples" while we're talking "oranges"? Scripture tells of a time when "darkness shall cover the earth, and deep darkness the people" (Isaiah 60: 2). Surely our world today is dark through misunderstanding God. His ways have appeared dark to us. For all the love attributed to Him in Scripture, how are we to understand those moments when His boundless *agape* gives way to unspeakable wrath? Could love find no better way to pay the wages of sin? God must deal with it, and He will. But how? The surprising Bible answer frees God from any blame whatever in the death of the unsaved and reveals him exactly like our perfect and perfectly harmless Lord Jesus (Hebrews 7:26).

Come with me now, on a journey through God's word, as we revisit the scenes of so many of the ages-old, mysterious judgments of God. As we push back the clouds of confusion that surround what appears to be His destructive side, we shall know as never before that "God is light and in Him is no darkness at all" (1 John 1:5).

In the spirit of intolerance Christ's foes opposed and tried to silence Him. That same spirit often manifests today wherever new thoughts threaten long-established views. Some bitterly condemn that which disturbs their preconceived ideas. But those with open minds, who persevere, who evaluate the consistency and Scriptural basis of this new model before allowing such prejudice to close their minds will be rewarded and, as others before them, may find themselves receiving it with joy.

And beyond the joy of this wonderful new picture of God lies another revelation, charged with solemn implications for our world today.

GOD'S PERFECT PORTRAIT

2

*"God is light, and in Him
is no darkness at all" (1 John 1:5).*

The human history of Jesus constitutes the complete revelation of God's character available for our study. All that God is, He was.

Jesus was "the brightness of His glory," the total statement of God sent forth to touch and bless our world, revealing to us the character of the Father. "For it is the God who commanded the light to shine out of darkness who has shone in our hearts to give the light of the knowledge of the glory [character] of God in the face of Jesus Christ" (Hebrews 1:3; 2 Corinthians 4:6. Also see Exodus 34:6.).

"I and My Father are one," Jesus said. One in nature, one in purpose, one in will. "He who has seen Me has seen the Father." "He who receives Me receives Him who sent Me" (John 10:30; 14:7-11;13:10).

God, As Jesus Revealed Him

Jesus revealed a creative, redemptive, healing God, who never brought needless pain to a sensitive soul. Even when, in love, He rebuked the leaders of His day, we can almost hear the tears in His voice, as He uttered His scathing words, which, rather than being destructive, were meant to redeem.

Startled by His disciples' suggestion that He call down fire upon the Samaritans who had slighted Him, He said, "Ye know not what manner of spirit ye are of" (Luke 9:55). What does this tell us about God? Would the fact that God performed such an act alter its "spirit"? Or is the evil nature of such an act eternally carved in granite—settled at all times, in all places, on all occasions? This event in our Lord's life suggests the latter. Burning humans in the name of religion is always and only the work of an *evil* spirit; Jesus insists it is not something our loving heavenly Father would do.

- 10 -

Jesus healed the ear of Malchus, the high priest's servant, gently rebuking Peter who had severed it with a sword, saying, "Put up again thy sword. . . All they that take the sword shall perish with the sword" (Matthew 26:52, KJV; also Revelation 13:10).

"Love your enemies," He said. "Bless those who curse you, do good to those who hate you, and pray for those who spitefully use you and persecute you." Why? *That you may be sons of your Father in heaven*" (Matthew 5: 44,45,). God the Father, Creator of the universe, as Jesus consistently presents Him, does not behave toward His enemies as other portions of Scripture seem to say. In the face of such apparent contradictions, we hear God saying, "Dig a little deeper in the word."

The Man, Christ Jesus

Jesus was a man's man who walked great distances on the dusty roads of ancient Palestine—traveling stretches for which we award prizes today, teaching vast multitudes, healing the sick, rebuking demons, standing his ground fearlessly before authority figures, telling them things they didn't want to hear, rising while others slept to spend time with His Father. If ever one were qualified by physical powers to command armies, it was He. Yet He declined the sword of earthly conquest held out to Him and chose instead the path to Calvary.

An Eye For An Eye?

"'You have heard that it was said, 'An eye for an eye and a tooth for a tooth,'" He said. "But I tell you not to resist an evil person. But whoever slaps you on your right cheek, turn the other to him also. If anyone wants to sue you and take away your tunic, let him have your cloak also. And whoever compels you to go one mile, go with him two. Give to him who asks you, and from him who wants to borrow from you do not turn away" (Matthew 5:38-42). Today people of depth and moral substance ponder this Man with awe. Whence came His intimate familiarity with the fine points of greatness? He carried the word of God built into His inner life. "He who is slow to anger is better than the mighty, and he who rules his spirit than he who takes a city" (Proverbs 16:32). Jesus—so sound as a human Being, so full of insight and peace and power—wouldn't descend to self-serving in His daily human interactions. He rose above those common instincts and, in benevolence and warmth toward all, kept on doing right.

Some have suggested that Jesus came the first time to show the kindly side of God, that when He returns in glory, He will then demonstrate His justice. However, nothing in the gospel record supports that view. Scripture says Jesus is the same "yesterday, today and forever" and that Deity doesn't change. (Hebrews 13:8; Malachi 3:6). God cannot and will not require humans to adhere to a standard He rejects for Himself. His commandments form not only the foundation of His government in heaven and on earth; they actually depict His character in words (see Psalm 97:2; 119:172; Jeremiah 23:6;33:16), as a novelist draws the inner life of protagonists with the pen. The principle which says "Thou shalt not kill," which Jesus expanded to mean Thou shalt not hate or damage in any way, originates in the heart of God.

Clearly, both the sixth commandment[5] and the example of Jesus combine to reveal a nondestructive God. This is an indisputable fact. There is a consistency, a harmony, an agreement between the law written down in the ten commandments and the law lived out in His life. It is the destructive events

---

[5]The sixth commandment states, "Thou shalt not kill" (Exodus 20:13, KJV) or as some Bible translations give it, "You shall not murder." Some have suggested that "murder" is the correct translation. They apparently believe this disproves the position of this book on God's character. But does the alternate translation "murder" in the sixth commandment solve anything?

"Murder" is said to mean the taking of human life in a willful, premeditated way. If Scripture ever depicts God as taking human life in a willful, premeditated way, then the commandment still does not transcribe His character with the word changed to "murder," and this solution flies out the window. Is God ever shown to take human life willfully or premeditatedly? What about Noah's flood? Sodom and Gomorrah? What about hell fire? And what does this solution say about humans taking human life? If it is not premeditated or willful, if it occurs in a moment of rage, then with the word changed to "murder" it would not violate the sixth commandment. This solution denies God the power to grant human victory over those acts of violence that occur in a "moment of passion."

Interestingly, some Bible students who are most opposed to the new translations of Scripture, stating they are more paraphrase than translation and reflect the bias of the translators, will throw out the King James Version rendering of this commandment as Thou shalt not kill in favor of You shall not murder, while railing against the new translations' presentation of virtually every other subject.

As often happens when we enter into quibbles such as this, debating the fine points of these two renderings removes us from a proper view of the "big picture." God would have us see the "preciousness" of human life. Not only is the physical life entitled to respect, but He would have us understand that the property, the reputation, the interests of others must be carefully protected as well. When we see that quality of grace in our God, how much more likely it is to transfer over to those who serve and admire Him. Finally, the original Hebrew word can be accurately translated either "kill" or "murder," with "kill" shown as the preferred rendering. As serious Bible students, we must beware of simplistic solutions that lead nowhere. No matter how "right" a solution appears on the surface, no matter how respected its champion, we owe our heavenly Father better service than to accept ideas out of hand, from regard for the persons offering them. Nothing will do but to sit down in a serious, prayerful way and actually study the subject through. Those who do so with a heart to know the truth will be rewarded.

described in Scripture that do not agree. Where two descriptions agree and a third is out of agreement, the obvious problem exists in the one that is out of agreement. The present work proposes to take Scriptural stories attributing destructive behavior to God and to bring them into harmony with the two standards of 1) the sixth commandment and 2) the character of Jesus. It can be done. But anyone who expects a pass for sin[6] is in for a big surprise.

Reviewing the life of our Lord from Bethlehem to the Mount of Olives, from which He ascended homeward to heaven, we find no evidence of the inclination to force allegiance to Himself, little we could interpret as destructive. "The Son of Man did not come to destroy men's lives, but to save them" (Luke 9:56). In fact, there was nothing in His life to correspond to a dark or destructive side in God. This no one can deny. Yet the life of Jesus holds insights into God's ultimate plans for dealing with the terrible problem of sin. And far more relevant than we have realized was a behavior of His little commented on up to now. When spurned or subjected to disrespect, He put the class in the strategy of walking away. Where our carnal humanity would wreak a powerful kind of vengeance on our tormentors, He who healed the sick and raised the dead, who had infinite resources at His disposal to deal with any enemy, gave us the example of His gracious habit of departing from where He was unwanted.

The God Who Goes Away

Jesus showed that God never forces His company on anyone. Time and again He demonstrated this important principle by the manner in which He lived. On one occasion some demons, which He rebuked out of two men, entered swine feeding nearby, causing the animals to rush over a cliff to their doom. This frightened onlookers and enraged the animals' owners. "And behold the whole city came out to meet Jesus. And when they saw Him, they begged Him to *withdraw* from their region. So He got into a boat, crossed over, and came to His own city" (Matthew 8:34; 9:1; Luke 8:37). No evidence of imposing His presence here unwanted. In this case as in so many others, Christ responds to rejection by departing.

Once when He healed on the Sabbath, "The Pharisees went out and began to plot against Him, discussing how to destroy Him. Jesus knew this and *withdrew* from the district." When He claimed the name "I Am," "they picked up stones to throw at Him, but Jesus hid Himself and *left* the temple" (Matthew 12:14, 15; Mark 3:6; John 8:59). Jesus' sole response to rejection was to go away. The cross says He would rather die Himself than destroy

---

[6]Sin is transgression of the law (1 John 3:4, KJV; Romans 5:13; 7:7).

His creatures.[7] However, He only "departed thence" when the citizens of a region made it clear they didn't want Him. Otherwise, Jesus was the essence of sociability.

He longed for the human touch, for human understanding and sympathy, for the warmth of friendship. He attended a wedding and there performed His first miracle by changing water into wine. He held children on His lap, healed the daughter of an outcast of Israel; beside Jacob's well He spoke publicly with a woman—and a Samaritan at that. He counted His friends among the wealthy and influential as well as among the poor and rejected, the sick and the lame. Whether appealing to His healing power or just sitting down in His loving presence, His friends knew Him as One who understood their need, who sympathized and would never withhold Himself.

We may today imagine Him, in His consummate courtesy, listening for our prayerful morning invitation and its hour-by-hour renewal, desirous that the listening universe know He is not encroaching upon our free will when, as our heavenly Guest, He comes in through His Spirit to abide and fellowship with us.

The Third Option

Besides revealing God as One who longs for human companionship but who will never force His presence on anyone, Jesus revealed a side of God which has delighted Christians through the centuries. He revealed Himself (and thus the Father) as Master of the Third Option.

The Pharisees, Sadducees, Herodians, and all the leadership groups of Christ's day had been enemies for years until He came along. His presence had a unifying effect upon them in their mutual passion to stamp out this heretic and his new faction. Repeatedly they tried to make Him say something of which they could accuse Him. They laid numerous traps for Him, where either way He answered, He lost. It was here, in scenes such as these, that He demonstrated His freedom from the limitations of average thinking.

A classic example involved a question they put to Him, "Is it lawful for us to pay taxes to Caesar or not?"

There were only two possible answers to this question, right? Yes or No.

If Jesus answered Yes, He would thereby express loyalty to the Roman government and alienate Israel, who resented Roman tribute more than

---

[7]According to the gospel, "all have sinned" (Romans 3:23), and "the wages of sin is death (Romans 6:23). This rule prevails throughout the universe of God. All humans who sin, then, receive the death sentence. Christ came to take that sentence upon Himself and to let the repentant sinner go free. The following pages will expand on this brief description

anything. But if He said No, He would make Himself unpopular with the Romans, a prospect involving some rather serious consequences.

Without hesitation Jesus called for a coin. "Whose inscription do you see?" He asked them. "They answered and said, Caesar's."

"Render therefore to Caesar the things that are Caesar's and unto God the things that are God's" (Luke 20:20-26). He not only had a third and better option but in expressing it He declared a timeless principle absolutely vital to human liberty. Thus Christians make the best citizens, civil authority honors the right of the individual to worship God according to his or her own conscience, and peace and harmony exist in society.

The Young Lawyer

In one of my favorite episodes of Christ's life, a bright young lawyer, the hope of the Pharisees, dressed for success in the robes and trappings of his station, came out to "test" the Master. Religion hasn't changed much through the years, it seems, for during that era various groups were forever arguing one point or other of religious dogma. One discussion centered upon which of the ten commandments was the most important. Therefore any commitment to one of those ten, while it might put you *in* with some, would put you *out* with most. And that is precisely the question the young man asked Jesus. "Which is the first commandment of all?"

These two young men faced off, Christ in His unpretending peasant's garb, the scribe's robes glittering in the sunlight. Which commandment would Jesus say? It didn't matter. Whatever reply He made would make Him many enemies.

"Jesus answered him, 'The first of all the commandments is: . . . You shall love the Lord your God with all your heart, with all your soul, with all your mind and with all your strength. This is the first commandment. And the second, like it, is this: You shall love your neighbor as yourself.' There is no commandment greater than these."

Jesus had another option. We may conclude, then, that God has options which we, in our humanness, simply cannot see.

The response of Jesus revealed His familiarity with the writings of Moses (Deuteronomy 6:5; Leviticus 19:18) and with something beyond the narrow arguments of unrenewed minds. The bright young lawyer caught the spirit of Christ's answer, revealing as it did the foundation upon which the law of God rests: supreme love to God and selfless service to humanity. And, seeing that, a bond with Christ formed in the young man's heart as he exclaimed, "'Well said, Teacher. You have spoken the truth, for there is one God and there is no other but He. And to love Him with all the heart, with all the understanding, with all the soul, and with all the strength, and to love one's neighbor as oneself is more than all the whole burnt offerings and sacrifices.'

"When Jesus saw that he answered wisely, he said to him, 'You are not far from the kingdom of God'" (Mark 12:28-34). What a look of understanding must have passed between them at that moment, when the world's status symbols yielded before the superiority of Christ's humble, heavenly insight!

Throughout the life of Jesus, this scenario repeated. He always had another idea. God has more options than we can conceive with our human understanding. Since He is not limited by our finite vision, let us not rule out the possibility that the "dark side" we always thought we saw in Him may yield to a brighter image, after all.

Christ and Anger

Multitudes of eager listeners sat before Him on a vast mountainside. Was He seated near the base with the people spread out above Him on a gradually inclining, grass-covered slope, like the seats in a giant amphitheater? Perhaps the sun shown warmly that day. Perhaps it was spring, with new buds and shoots appearing on the surrounding foliage. Perhaps birds blessed the air with cheerful songs and lilies bloomed, as our Savior began to teach, revealing the kingdom of heaven as a paradoxical land at odds with earthly ways. Blessed are the poor, the meek, the merciful, He said. "Blessed are you when they revile and persecute you, and say all kinds of evil against you falsely for My sake" (Matthew 5:11). Tenderly but firmly, He taught them that earth has little use for much that heaven values.

"You have heard that it was said to those of old, 'You shall not murder.' and whoever murders will be in danger of the judgment. But I say to you that whoever is angry with his brother without a cause shall be in danger of the judgment" (Matthew 5:21, 22). Clearly, Jesus meant to discourage not only murder but the emotion that leads to it. He taught that true obedience to the commandments of God requires more than surface work; it requires a principle lodged deep within the inner human spirit.

"Without a cause?" What "cause" would Christ consider sufficient to warrant an angry reaction? What kinds of provocations elicited an angry response from Him, thus modeling for us justifiable human anger or destructive behavior? Only three incidents in His entire life offer insights here: Twice He cleansed the temple; once He cursed a fig tree.

In cleansing the temple, yes, He expressed great outrage. He thus gave us an example that when we see God dishonored, we have cause for "righteous indignation" and for action. He made a whip, but we have no record that He used it on anyone; indeed, He likely used it to herd the cattle and sheep, and the humans merely swept out with the flow. It was not the whip in His hand as much as the authority in His voice and manner that caused the moneychangers to flee. Jesus didn't kill anyone; He didn't touch anyone, so far as the record states. The guilty fled from the temple as the guilty always flee from the threat of exposure and retribution. (See Matthew 21:12-17; John 2:13-17.)

Similarly, in cursing the fig tree He revealed the opposite of a destructive spirit.

Jesus had an insight, which found expression in the things of nature and in all of life around Him. He saw eternal lessons in flowers and birds, in sheep and shepherds. When He sought upon a leafy fig tree fruit to satisfy His hunger and found none, He must have thought to Himself, That's just like . . .

And so He gave the tree human qualities and used it to illustrate a truth of His kingdom. That tree looked like a fig tree. It had leaves like a fig tree, and seemed for all the world like one. But a fig tree bears fruit. Without the fruit it is a worthless pretender.

How like religion, He must have thought. All those leaves, all that pretension, but no fruit. In cursing the fig tree, He illustrated the fate of those who rest in a form of godliness but whose lives display no spiritual fruit, whose religion consists of observing ritual and talking 'God talk' but whose ethics fail in their private moments. Rather than chop the tree down and burn it, He ceased to sustain it and it withered, because apart from God's sustenance there is no life. (See Matthew 21:19; Luke 3:9.)

The Doctrine of Substitution

Far from destructive, Jesus came that we might have life and have it more abundantly than we could possibly have it without Him. He planned a greater depth, fullness and quality to life than even most Christians realize. The life He gave involved Him in our own life, and ours in His, in an intimate way strangely unknown in the Christian world. Yet it is the very heart of the gospel. Where known, it is called the Doctrine of Substitution— the higher (no, highest) education of Christendom. Christ's delay in fulfilling His promise to return to this earth may stem from our "illiteracy" regarding this concept and thus our failure to live in it. We cannot confront the dynamics of eternal reward and punishment without understanding this truth.

Before learning this doctrine had a name, Substitution, I called it "Identification," and I am still not convinced that mine is not the better title, since the concept involves Christ's absolute and full identification with those He came to save and our absolute and full identification with Him in His humanity. What would make such intimate connection essential in the plan of redemption?

Let's say a young man commits a crime for which the compulsory penalty is death. But his mother loves him and appeals to the judge to allow her to pay the price for his crime. How would the judge respond?

"Mother," he might say, "I can see you deeply love your son. But I am not authorized to pass his sentence on to you. The punishment is always attached to the crime. It is called 'consequences.' If he does the crime and you take the consequences, justice will be turned on its ear. No, I am sorry. It cannot be done." Scripture itself recognizes this principle in Deuteronomy 24:16 (See also Ezekiel 18:20).

In like manner, neither is God authorized to pass the penalty of transgression on to Anyone—except the guilty party. If the plan of redemption were to work, a way had to be found in which to *blend* the sinner with the Sin Bearer, the human with the divine.

The Exchange

When Jesus came to live and die upon this earth, He did not merely come for us or on our behalf; oh, no. He came "as us." This distinction involves more than semantic hair splitting. When God looked at Him, He saw me; He saw you. In fact, in the Father's sight Christ was the corporate human. He came *as* every person born into this world. Though He never ceased to be God, Scripture says He "emptied Himself" (Philippians 2:7, JB) of His divine powers and privileges, retaining only His power to forgive sin, and walked the earth fully human, as you and I must walk it, and experienced life as we experience it. Had He not fully identified with fallen humanity, had He not fully become human (except that He didn't sin), Satan would have been the first to cry "foul!" when God accepted His substitutionary life and death for this world. The enemy would have charged that the achievements of a Superior Being could not fairly substitute for the failures of a fallen one.When we sanitize Christ's humanity, allegedly to honor and glorify Him, it frankly does the opposite. It obscures our understanding of the magnificence of His performance as the Lamb of God. It knocks a few rungs off the bottom of the heavenly ladder,[8] preventing it from reaching down to you and me.[9]

---

[8]Genesis 28:12; John 1:51.

[9]The experience of Jesus, clothed in our fallen nature yet victorious over sin assures us that no matter how bad our case we too can have victory. Are we sinless? Are we righteous? No. We are "wretched, miserable, poor, blind and naked" (Rev. 3:17). But if we practice our surrender, the powerful Holy Spirit can still come in and live out heaven's ways in us. The only righteousness available to us is His. The Bible is clear. Righteousness is a Person (Jeremiah 23:6; 33:16; Hebrews 2:14-18; Romans 1:3).

Our Master took upon His divinity our fallen human nature. As one of us, and with our human equipment, He lived out for us a perfect history and a perfect example, leaving the enemy no legitimate ground on which to challenge the Atonement. If Jesus had possessed any advantage over us in achieving this triumph, it would have disqualified Him as our Redeemer, and Satan would have exulted. Heaven could not credit His victory to us, unless He came in our shoes.

But what may be even less known is that the gift of eternal life He brought comes only with Himself. He said, "Unless you eat the flesh of the Son of Man and drink His blood, you have no life in you" (John 6:53). Jesus made it clear in this passage that His flesh and blood were *His words*, and their power to bring Him through the Holy Spirit into human lives as a living though invisible reality. Through that presence He would change our thinking into paths unknown upon earth, but fully known in the kingdom of God. Only thus can we be holy, for it is His holiness. Only thus can we be truly wise, in His wisdom. Only thus can we, lost sinners, cease to sin. Never will we be anything but lost sinners, except *in Him* and the righteousness He brings to us.

The human Jesus could not live righteously of Himself. "The Son can do nothing of Himself"; "the Father who dwells in Me does the works" (John 5: 19; 14:10). Fallen humanity cannot be righteous, but Christ was righteous in the fallen humanity He took. What was the secret of His power? It appears the Father lived in Him by the divine Spirit. He, like his cousin, John the Baptist, was filled with the Holy Ghost from before his birth (See Luke 1:15). But unlike John,[10] Jesus enjoyed unbroken union with the Holy Spirit. This connection enabled Him to live above the clamors of the fallen humanity He assumed in the Incarnation. True, it was borrowed but true righteousness nonetheless. And not only did Christ require this union to maintain a victorious humanity, it is a connection available to and vital for humans who would be saved. "If when we were enemies we were reconciled to God through the death of His Son, much more, having been reconciled, we shall be saved by His life [in us]" (Romans 5:10).

He, as the corporate human, showed us that holiness for humans takes two, God and us. If we as Christians have failed to live up to God's standard, it is because we have failed to understand our desperate and ceaseless need for the living presence of Jesus Christ, through His Spirit and His word, in our lives every moment of every day. Right living, right doing, righteousness,

---

[10]Although we have no specific information about John's participation in sin, Scripture tells us, "There is none righteous, no not one [human]," and "All have sinned" (Romans 3:10,23.)

holiness—these belong only to God. Humans have access to them only while living *in Him*, consciously aware of His abiding presence.

Since Christ's return to heaven, He has sent the Holy Spirit as His representative to be our personal Companion, just as He came representing the Father and as the Holy Spirit represented the Father in Him. We cannot accept His gift of salvation without accepting Him, in the person of His Spirit, to walk with us and be Master of our soul day by day. Through Scripture He counsels us of His will, but our victory as Christians, our power to do right, centers on staying in communion companionship with Him, for it is this union, this connection, that saves. When we realize His presence, Scripture provides the knowledge and He provides the power to do right. It is then possible to do right and hard to do wrong, for who would not do right in His presence? In saving oneness with Him, conscious, always conscious of His nearness, the sharp edges disappear from righteous living, and the "beauty of [His] holiness" appears (Psalm 96:9).

But He has done more. "God, who is rich in mercy, because of His great love with which He loved us, even when we were dead in trespasses [He provided for us before we chose to follow Him], made us alive together with Christ (by grace you have been saved), and raised us up together, and made us sit together in heavenly places in Christ Jesus, that in the ages to come He might show the exceeding riches of His grace in His kindness toward us in Christ Jesus" (Ephesians 2:4-7). We were in Christ in His earthly life, in His death, and those who consent to hide their lives in Him He will finally exalt to eternal heavenly places.

The Atonement

But we may so fully enter into our Lord's life only because He so fully entered into ours. We have sinned, and the Bible says, "The wages of sin is death" (Romans 6:23). In order to be fully ethical and demonstrate the consistency and predictability essential to the security of His creatures, God must fulfill His word. Somebody had to die for our sins. Ordinarily, it would be us.

But God had another idea.

In order to understand how God intends to deal with sin, we must look at how He dealt with His own Son, Jesus Christ, the great Sin-bearer.

Jesus laid aside His divine privileges and lived, as we may live, in the Father through the Spirit during His pilgrimage on earth. His was a constant companionship, a constant communion and fellowship with the Father, until about the time He entered the Garden of Gethsemane, when the sins of a rebel world began to roll upon Him. Still in His role as the corporate human, a change began. At this point, as the apostle Paul said, God made Him to be sin for us (2 Corinthians 5:21).

Since Jesus lived as one of us, He also died as one of us. He took my death and yours. Whereas He took the death penalty for the entire human race, most people (sadly and unnecessarily) will insist upon receiving their own penalty. Therefore, Christ's death holds insights into the nature of the final destruction of the lost. God could not allow the death of Christ to be one way and the death of everyone else to be another way and still apply Christ's death to the account of the saved. They must be equal, in nature rather than circumstances. God the Father's role must be the same in both cases.

Christ's death was the sinner's death. But God did not come down to the cross and personally execute Him. Rather, when the sins of the world rolled on Jesus in Gethsemane, the sense of His Father's presence began to recede. God the Father now treated His Son as a lost sinner, deprived Him of the sense of His sustaining nearness, drawing forth from His wounded heart the anguished cry from the cross, "My God, my God, why hast thou forsaken me?" (Matthew 27:47; Mark 15:34, KJV). Though sinless still, He bore the sin of a world and the Father's drawing away from that sin. Just as human rejection caused Christ to withdraw in His earthly life, His role as the Embodiment of sinful rebellion against God caused the Father to withdraw from *Him* in Gethsemane and on Calvary. But God never touched Him in cruel violence. Rather, He *withdrew* from His Son (now Sin Personified) and released Him into the hands of the destructive forces surrounding Him. Those forces had followed Christ from His earliest moments but always without success until now, when God "made Him to be sin for us" and let Him go.

Who Delivered Christ to Die?

Christ tried to share this prospect with His disciples and thus prepare them for the approaching crisis. "For He taught His disciples and said to them, 'The Son of Man is being delivered into the hands of men, and they will kill Him.'" "Behold, we are going up to Jerusalem and the Son of Man will be delivered to the chief priests and to the scribes, and they will condemn Him to death" (Mark 9:31; 10:33). Who was "delivering" Him? Judas certainly planned to, but Jesus did not refer to him. The apostle Paul makes clear who "delivered Him up":

"He that spared not his own Son, but delivered Him up for us all, how shall he not with him also freely give us all things?" (Romans 8:32, KJV; Romans 4:24, 25). It was the Father who delivered Him (or released Him) to the destructive forces around Him. (See also Matthew 26:2, 14, 15; 27:18; Mark 10:33, 34; 14:10; 15:1, 11; Luke 22:4; Acts 2:23.)

Significantly, Pilate also "delivered" Christ to be crucified. But not before our Lord informed the proud ruler he would have no power to do this if God did not allow it (John 19:11). There can be no question that God's role in the punishment of the Sin-bearer was to withdraw and hand him over or release him to the power of destruction, but not to perform the execution itself. . . .

Even though He says He did!

> "'Awake, O sword, against My Shepherd,
> Against the Man who is My Companion,'
> says the Lord of hosts.
> 'Strike the Shepherd,
> and the sheep will be scattered.'"
> (Zechariah 13:7)

Jesus claims these words as a prophecy of Himself: "Then Jesus said to them [His disciples], 'all of you will be made to stumble because of Me this night, for it is written: I will strike the Shepherd, and the sheep of the flock will be scattered'" (Matthew 26:32; Mark 14:27). Both Father and Son agree; God claims to "strike" Christ, although we would certainly not describe it that way. The Old Testament prophecy from which He quotes also suggests use of a "sword," or violence, "Against the Man who is My Companion," a clear reference to the intimacy of relationship between Father and Son. Yes, Christ died violently, but we would not say by His Father's hand.

In Isaiah 53, universally accepted within Christendom as a Messianic prophecy, Scripture says, "Surely He has borne our griefs and carried our sorrows; yet we esteemed Him stricken, *smitten of God* and afflicted" (v. 4).

Does God consider the removal of Himself from humans as an act of aggression against them? Christ, the corporate human, died when God withdrew from Him and released Him to destruction. Yet God insists He "struck" His Son. Is this how God strikes? By withdrawing and releasing humans to the destructive forces around them? Would this model fit other situations? And if it would, why would God choose to describe Himself as the agent of execution?

Jerusalem Destroyed

In searching Christ's life for clues of God's role in the punishment of sinners, we find one incident particularly meaningful. For centuries God had sent prophets to Israel to warn them of the consequences of their entrenched rebellion against heaven and to plead with them to repent.

But, as Christ sat upon a colt on Olivet's brow one of the last evenings before His death, He looked out over the beautiful city of Jerusalem and vept, because He knew the people would shortly seal their centuries-long ejection of heaven through His own crucifixion. He saw the armies of Titus besiege the city some forty years hence, saw indescribable woe descend upon he people, saw the temple of God in flames unquenchable through any human effort.

And He saw more. He knew the interplay of invisible forces that would finally open the door to this catastrophe, and He wept. His thoughts found expression soon in a confrontation with the nation's religious leaders.

"O Jerusalem, Jerusalem, the one who kills the prophets and stones those who are sent to her! How often I wanted to gather your children together, as a hen gathers her chicks, under her wings, but you were not willing" (Matthew 23:37).

Jerusalem perished when she, through Christ's crucifixion, abandoned connection with God. The symbol of a protecting parent bird, usually an eagle, spreading wings over its young, abounds in Scripture, denoting the relationship between God and His people and their dependence upon the heavenly provision available only in that connection. It is perhaps the nearest heaven can come to describing invisible realities in human language. But it is by no means the only symbol in Scripture clearly representing this same truth.

HOW THE BIBLE EXPLAINS ITSELF

3

"For precept must be upon precept,
precept upon precept; line upon line, line upon line,
here a little, and there a little" (Isaiah 28:10).

Imagine, if you will, that you live in a land where the word "tooth" means "tree stump." If you journey to my world and attempt to get your tree stump uprooted, you might get some interesting looks when you ask, "May I use your tractor to uproot my tooth?" How much progress would you make with this project until you learn to speak in the local tongue? Likewise, our difficulty in seeing the Bible picture of God is a language problem—a problem easily cleared up when some careful comparisons are made within the text of the Word itself.

In order to lay a foundation for discussing specific incidents of God's vengeance we must first look at some idiosyncrasies of Scripture which reveal how God expresses Himself. In so doing we shall delve into some related themes. These are not digressions. All the issues of redemption intersect in the character of God; therefore, touching on these related themes, besides showing some peculiarities of Scripture, will also help unravel the mystery of God's role in the destructive acts attributed to Him in Scripture.

Paradoxical Principles

First, it is often necessary to think in opposites to understand many truths of the kingdom of God. No one will ever know God, as He desires to be known, until we begin to think and live by God's paradoxical principles. Of the numerous examples in Scripture, we shall examine only a few.

- He who loves his life will lose it, and he who hates his life in this world will keep it for eternal life" (John 12:25).

- "To everyone who has will be given, and from him who does not have, even what he has will be taken away from him (Luke 19:26).

- God has chosen the foolish things of the world to put to shame the wise, and God has chosen the weak things of the world to put to shame the things which are mighty; and the base things of the world and the things which are despised God has chosen, and the things which are not, to bring to nothing the things that are (1 Corinthians 1:27, 28).

- Through death He . . . destroy[ed] . . . the devil (Hebrews 2:14).

The abundance of these apparent paradoxes in Scripture says something about God's mind vital to the present topic. "My thoughts are not your thoughts, nor are your ways My ways, says the Lord" (Isaiah 55:8,9). Public opinion rarely reflects the mind of God. Therefore, we should not be surprised to discover we have misunderstood in the arena of God's "vengeance" as in so many others.

Be careful here; this perspective could be carried to excess. Accept only what the Bible clearly supports. The point is we should not be shocked to find heavenly truth in reverse of popular ideas.

In view of "divine retribution" as *Christ's life* expressed it, we might well ask whether there is more to understand on this point as well. Does truth on this topic lie somewhere opposite the place we always thought? Perhaps.

Other Biblical idiosyncrasies bear upon this topic and demand notice.

Biblical Contradictions

A fact upon which skeptics lean heavily and which Christians cannot deny is that the Bible often seems like an encyclopedia of contradictions. Failure to harmonize these problems has fragmented Christendom, in itself testifying against us to the secular mind. At its worst these apparent contradictions have led to actual persecution through economic sanctions and even death laws, as one side gains political clout and uses it to promote religious ideology. In laying a foundation for discussing specific incidents of God's vengeance, we must deal with these apparent Biblical contradictions, since they address the primary issue.

Let us take as our first example a prominent argument in Christendom, the issue of how law (works/obedience) and grace (faith) apply to our salvation. Some groups say we are saved by grace through faith, basing their belief on such texts as:

- By grace you have been saved through faith, and that not of yourselves; it is the gift of God, *not of works*, lest anyone should boast (Ephesians 2:8,9).

- A man is not justified by the works of the law but by faith in Jesus Christ, even we have believed in Christ Jesus, that we might be justified by faith in Christ and not by the works of the law; for *by the works of the law no flesh shall be justified* (Galatians 2:16).

Although Scripturally there can be no doubt God grants salvation as a free gift not contingent upon good deeds, the incomplete understanding of this truth has produced problems. It has fostered antinomianism, the idea that salvation hinges only upon accepting and professing Christ, and lifestyle/works don't matter. Despite its apparently Scriptural basis, it doesn't take much imagination to see some problems with this view from a practical standpoint. Principally, it opens the door to spiritual anarchy and blurs the distinction between right and wrong, making them dependent upon individual interpretation.

On the other side of the picture we have this:

- And I saw the dead, small and great, standing before God, and the books were opened. And another book was opened, which is the Book of Life. And the dead were *judged according to their works,* by the things which were written in the books. The sea gave up the dead who were in it, and Death and Hades delivered up the dead who were in them. And they were judged, each one *according to his works* (Revelation 20:12, 13).

- Faith without works is dead. . . . A man is *justified by works*, and not by faith only (James 2:20, 24).

No one can say that the Bible does not stress works. The voice of God cries out in the Old Testament and New, admonishing His people to good works. And the works enjoined in Scripture require more than just being nice. They demand living against human nature, higher and better than humanly possible, as high in fact as the kingdom of God is higher than the kingdoms of this world. They demand a change of mind, a change of values, priorities, interests, a very dying to this world. In short, the works enjoined in Scripture cannot be done by humans. And there's the rub.

So here we have a classic Scriptural contradiction. And how do Christians deal with it and with other similar cases? Do they study through in the spirit of sincere inquiry and harmonize these issues? Usually, no. Rather, these apparent problems can become the basis for argument, alienation and division within Christendom.

None of this need happen, if Christians determined to harmonize these apparent contradictions through earnest Bible study, allowing Scripture to be its own interpreter, until a clear picture emerges of the truth of the matter. What a blessed day it would be in Christendom, if we could meet together as brothers and sisters in the Lord and tackle these difficult topics in just that spirit!

Juxtaposing ideas sometimes helps to clarify; therefore, at this point we shall introduce a format that will become familiar as we move along.

How Does God Save Humans

One Perspective	Another Perspective
By grace you have been saved through faith, and that not of yourselves; it is the gift of God, *not of works*, lest anyone should boast (Eph. 2:8, 9).	Faith without works is dead. . . . A man is *justified by works* and not by faith alone (James 2:20, 24).

Each reference represents an abundant body of Scripture saying the same thing. In this case we are fortunate in having a third set of references that harmonize this apparent contradiction:

How Does God Save Humans

One Perspective	Another Perspective
By grace you have been saved through faith, and that not of yourselves; it is the gift of God, *not of works*, lest anyone should boast (Eph. 2:8, 9).	Faith without works is dead. . . . A man is *justified by works* and not by faith alone (James 2:20, 24).

Comment

For in Jesus Christ neither circumcision [works] availeth anything, nor uncircumcision [faith]; but *faith which worketh by love* (Galatians 5:6, KJV).

Galatians 5:6 defines saving faith as a faith which "works" through a special kind of other-centered love called *agape*. Therefore, the works which humans cannot generate, in and of themselves, flow out of the life powered by genuine faith. When heaven looks at a life and sees the "beauty of holiness" expressed in reverence for God, sensitivity to others' needs and feelings, and the ability to rise above the harmful instincts of our human nature, they know Someone else lives there besides the human and His are the works they see. Paul in Galatians 2:16, KJV, calls this "the faith of Jesus Christ," or we might say, Jesus living out His faith in the believer. This faith works, and the faith that works is the faith that saves.

The writings of Paul the apostle are sometimes hard to understand principally because we have not understood this model, which forms the very core of his message.

How does God save? He saves humans in faith oneness with Himself; the works merely show that the union exists. When God sees more evidence of His Spirit than of us, walking in our shoes, He credits us with the history of our Companion, as He laid our history upon Him on Calvary so long ago. More than that, He changes our mind about everything the world and our own sinful nature have taught us and enables us to live the heavenly way, thus fitting us for eternal life in His kingdom.

The Atonement

This model is God's ideal for us; He calls it the *Atonement,* or At-one-ment, the bringing of humans back into oneness with Himself. (See John 17: 20-23.) Toward this end He constantly draws us and seeks to educate our minds. Although He has experienced mixed success through the centuries, He has never been without those who lived *in Him*, and prophecy is clear that before His return He will have *a people* who understand and live in this, His ideal will.

The Role of Law

But how do we know if we are living in Him or in a fantasy world? That's where God's law comes in. Scripture makes clear that works, obedience, law-keeping play a role in the gospel (See, for example, Revelation 14, especially verses 6 and 12, which places the law and the gospel together in an end-time setting.)

A kingdom, by definition, requires a foundational body of law to provide security to its citizens and to facilitate their interactions. God's kingdom is no exception. Whereas the Bible came principally from the hand of prophets, the simple and concise law governing His kingdom was too important to give to the world through human hands. With His own finger God carved its principles upon tables of stone, signifying their eternal permanence. It is true, God's presence in the human brings righteousness, but it is also true that while living in Him and still possessing free will, humans need a sin detector or standard of behavior to govern their decision making and to gauge whether they are living His way; that is, whether they are true fruit bearing branches of the living Vine (John 15:1-8) or mere pretenders. And God graciously gave the world that standard in the ten commandments.[11]

Recently some in various branches of government endorsed their importance by trying to have the ten commandments hung in school rooms and other public buildings across the country. A controversial endeavor, yes, and particularly puzzling when so many professed Christians insist that the ten commandments were somehow cancelled, nailed to the cross, along with the ceremonial law of symbols and sacrifices.

Indeed, some Christians take the position that, because the righteous works described in the ten commandments have no saving merit (which they do not), they have no use at all, and that the more contempt they place upon the law of God, the more commendable they are in His sight. It's hard to take that position seriously. In our world awash in evil can we afford to jettison the ten commandments as a standard of responsible behavior?

And, amazingly, these very Christians are often the first to applaud the efforts of civil government to shore up the damage done by their own clergy, who, gravely derelict in duty, search Scripture with a microscope, as many have done, looking for loopholes and dredging up missiles to hurl *against* the ten commandments, instead of thundering their eternal permanence from every pulpit in the land. What a confusing state of things! Civil government trading roles with Christianity—passing human laws to rescue Christianity's failure to persuade. If a possibility existed that God's law could be set aside, would heaven not have seized upon it the moment sin entered, rather than surrendering its mighty Commander to die to atone for the law's transgression?

The ten commandments are actually a written description of God's character (Compare Jeremiah 23:6 and 33:16 with Psalm 119:172 and Isaiah 51:7), and their purpose is to show us our need for Christ (Galatians 3:24), who shares with us His own righteousness. God is the origin and source of those ten principles. Thus, the ten commandments inform us, but the Lord Our Righteousness, living within, empowers us. He is the living law. If we would walk with Him, we must agree to let Him change us into His own likeness of character, in order to blend our characters into His own.

God is love. The cross of Christ reveals it. How can the human heart respond to that love with anything less? And love, in its purest form, seeks the happiness of its object. Perhaps surpassing all other reasons to honor God's commandments is that Jesus said our doing so would make Him

---

[11]Jesus says we will know the true Christian "by his fruits" (Matt. 7:20; Gal. 5:22, 23). The law of God serves as the fruit-checker, whereby Christians and their associates gauge the reality of the believer's oneness with Christ through the Holy Spirit. If the experience is real, the fruit will be there.

happy. "If you love Me," He said, "keep My commandments (John 14:15). To Jesus, obedience is the litmus test of love.

When we walk in fellowship with Him, His ways, as set out in that holy law, seem beautiful and desirable. It takes converted eyes to see this; therefore, our attitude toward His ten commandments reveals whether we have been "born again" (John 3:3). It can be seen, then, that obedience to those ten principles is, ultimately, about protecting our relationship with God, not so much about being saved. As day by day we abide in Him, "being saved" takes care of itself.

Sabbath observance, at the very heart of God's law, symbolizes the reality of this experience in our lives (Exodus 31:12, 13; Ezekiel 20:12, 20). It means "rest" from leaning on our own works of righteousness. It is the ultimate symbol of re-creation, rest in the Lord and living by faith.

Biblical Contradictions

Some may wonder what all this has to do with how God punishes the wicked, so slowly do we comprehend the interrelationship of truth. A little reflection will show that if God saves humans through reunion with Himself, authenticated by obedience to His commandments, then punishment or eternal loss is the consequence of failure to enter into reunion. To avoid the punishment, we need to understand and experience the alternative.

Further, we have seen what to do with Biblical contradictions. If we stack all the texts supporting Proposition A over here, and all the texts supporting Proposition B over there, the idea is not to take our pick and ignore the rest, as we are wont to do. Rather, knowing God does not contradict Himself, we continue studying until we resolve the issue into a unity of truth, until we see the full picture *all* the texts convey. In seeking to know the mind of God on any topic, until we have logically and Scripturally resolved evidence in contrast with our personal view, we cannot be sure we have arrived at truth, on which the weight of public opinion has no bearing whatsoever. What must God think of our failure to follow this simple plan?

Following are just a few of the perplexing apparent contradictions, which have puzzled students of Scripture for years. Studying them provides insight into the way God sometimes expresses Himself and reveals a principle we may use in understanding God's alleged dark side.

Who sends a lying spirit

One Perspective	Another Perspective
The Lord said, "Who will persuade Ahab to go up that he may fall at Ramoth Gilead?" . . . A spirit came forward and stood before theLord and said . . . "I will go out and be a lying spirit in the mouth of all the prophets" (1 Kings 22:20, 22).	It is impossible for God to lie . . . God . . . cannot lie (Hebrews 6:18;Titus1:2).

We have no Scriptural clarification on this point. Next question:

Who Led David To Number Israel

One Perspective	Another Perspective
The anger of the Lord was aroused against Israel and *He* moved David . . . to . . . number Israel and Judah (2 Sam. 24:2)	Now *Satan* stood up against Israel and movedDavid to number Israel (1 Chron. 21:1)

Again, we have no clarifying comment. We only know from Scripture that God punished David for this action (1 Chronicles 21:14), strongly suggesting that, as humans would express it, He had nothing to do with David's decision to initiate a census in Israel. But if God did not move David to "number Israel," *why does He say He did?*

Who Killed Saul?

One Perspective	Another Perspective
So Saul died for his unfaithfulness which he had committed against the Lord, because he did not keep the word of the Lord, and also because he consulted a medium for guidance but he did not inquire of the Lord; therefore *He [God]* killed him, and turned the kingdom over to David, the son of Jesse(1 Chron. 10:13,14)	Saul said to his armorbearer, "Draw your sword, and thrust me through with it". . . But his armorbearer would not. . . . Therefore, *Saul* took a sword and fell on it. . . So Saul . . . died (1 Chron. 10:4, 6).

Who Hardened Pharoah's Heart?

One Perspective	Another Perspective
And the Lord said to Moses, "When you go back to Egypt, see that you do all those wonders before Pharoah which I have put in your hand. But *I will harden his heart* so that he will not let the people go" (Exodus 4:21).	But when Pharoah saw that there was relief, he hardened his heart and did not heed them, as the Lord had said . . . But *Pharoah hardened his heart* at this time also; neither would he let the people go (Exodus 8:14, 32).

Is God Furious?

One Perspective	Another Perspective
I am full of the fury of the Lord (Jeremiah 6:11).	Fury is not in Me [says the Lord] (Isaiah 27:4).

Here God seems to take responsibility for things He did not actually do. Why? We have no clarifying Biblical comment.

No specific "counterpoint" statements exist for these nonetheless puzzling declarations:

•But the Spirit of the Lord departed from Saul, and an evil spirit *from the Lord* troubled him (1 Samuel 16:14, KJV;).

• God will send them [the wicked] strong delusion (2 Thessalonians 2:11).

• I [God] create calamity (Isaiah 45:7).

• I the Lord have [margin: 'misled'] that prophet (Ezekiel 14:9).

While most of these statements express the problem, a few hint of a solution:

Who Killed the Firstborn of Egypt?

One Perspective	Another Perspective
God speaking: "For *I* will pass through the land of Egypt on that night and will strike all the firstborn in the land of Egypt, both man and beast; against all the gods of Egypt *I* will execute judgment: I am the Lord" (Exodus 12:12).	For the Lord will pass through to strike the Egyptians: and when He sees the blood on the doorposts, the Lord will pass over the door and not allow *the destroyer* to come into your houses to strike you (Exodus 12:23).

What Was the Father's Role In the Death of Jesus?

One Perspective	Another Perspective
I [God] will strike the Shepherd. . . . We esteemed Him stricken, *smitten by God*(Mark 14:27; Isaiah 53:4).	My God, My God, why have You *forsaken* Me?(Mark 15:34).

We have already noted that God did not execute Christ, but we still have that puzzling language stating He did. What can it mean? We shall now put these last two pairs on "hold" until the next chapter, since we must cover more background in order to better assess their bearing on the issue.

However, let me at this point suggest a simple governing principle by which we may understand such statements. As we proceed, we shall test its validity:

Principle: God sees and describes Himself as *doing* what He does not prevent.

Since God could have prevented these incidents but chose not to do so, He depicts Himself as the actual instrument or performing agent. Note how often He describes them as His own doing in vivid, convincing terms. Yet we are justified, if they do not make sense in terms of the total picture or in terms of God's character *as Christ expressed it*, to wonder if He simply could have but didn't prevent it.

Why would God choose to so express Himself? His reason is not unknown in the human realm.

The Blame-taker vs. the Accuser

Some time back I worked in an office for a usually very fair-minded man. But one day he got the idea I had not forwarded an important report on its due date. I had no recollection of anyone telling me to send that report out; however, I quickly prepared it for forwarding and wrote a cover memorandum taking full responsibility for its tardiness. When I showed it to the boss for his approval, he trashed it. "In this office we don't get into blame placing," he said. "As director and manager of this office, I am responsible for all the work that's done here." And he quickly re-wrote the memo.

The story has a happy ending. In a matter of minutes he realized he had looked at the wrong report, which was not supposed to go anywhere, and he graciously apologized to me.

But even as it happened I saw something of God's mind when the boss took the blame. Maturity understands the importance of assuming responsibility, while immaturity blames everything and everyone in sight. Thus our supremely mature God makes Himself ultimately responsible for the results of granting His intelligent creatures free will, even to the extent of assuming blame for the numerous episodes of destructive acts attributed to Him in Scripture—acts He had no authority to prevent.

Our heavenly Father assures us *He is in charge of His universe*. As Creator of heavens and earth and Sustainer of life in the universe, He will never give Satan equal billing with Himself—will never point a finger and say, "He did it!" Since God could have prevented an incident but, out of respect for His creatures' free will, chose not to do so, He sees and often describes *Himself* as *doing* it.

4

The history of civilization is a history of war. From ancient battles of forgotten kings to 20th century superpower conflicts, each succeeding generation has mobilized its armies on the field of confrontation.

This conflict theme pervades the pages of Holy Writ. Its stories make up episodes in a context of warfare on a cosmic scale, and Scripture tells us where it all began.

"War broke out in heaven: Michael and his angels fought against the dragon; and the dragon and his angels fought, but they did not prevail, nor was a place found for them in heaven any longer" (Revelation 12:7, 8). Scripture places God's vengeance and the rise and fall of nations within this conflict setting.

"I will be like the Most High," said Lucifer—before his fall, "son of the morning" (Isaiah 14:12, 14), but afterward "the dragon." According to the Bible, war began as an ideological conflict between the Creator God and one who aspired to His office. "In righteousness He [God] doth judge and make war" (Revelation 19:11).[12] The weapons in this contest were truth on God's side and deception on the side of His adversary, and when deception no longer moved the minds of heaven's intelligences, this would-be deity had to find another home.

Revelation 12 says a third of the angels fell and were "cast out"; Jude 6 says they "left," but no one says anyone was "killed." Not so when Lucifer and his host plummeted to our world and the ideological war that commenced in heaven became a synonym for deadly force, continuing in blood that great conflict which began in envy and persists today, not only on fields of earthly battle but also in the minds and daily moral choices of every man and woman on this planet.

God plays the leading role in the drama, not only as Creator but also as Sustainer of all life and order in the universe. "It is He [God] who gives

---

[12]"Righteousness" is conformity to God's commandments (Psalm 119:172), including the sixth. Thus, the heavenly warfare could not have involved killing.

everything, including life and breath, to everyone. . . . It is in Him that we live and move and exist" (Acts 17:25, 28). He sustains life in two ways: first, through the presence of His Holy Spirit in our world and, secondly, through the activities of holy angels, supporting players stationed here with a commission to protect the earth.

Ministry of Angels

Paul the apostle says, "[Angels] are all spirits whose work is service sent to help those who will be heirs of salvation" (Hebrews 1:14). Since God planned and provided for the salvation of all, we are all recipients of the ministry of holy angels.

Zechariah 6 describes four symbolic horse-drawn chariots advancing from before God's throne toward earth, to pass through or patrol the four points of the compass. "Who are they?" asks the prophet.

They are four "spirits" of heaven, he learns. Notice in Hebrews Paul calls angels "spirits."[13] Psalm 68:17, KJV, verifies that these chariots symbolize angels. "The chariots of God are twenty thousand, even thousands of angels."

By their dispersion to all points of the compass the prophet conveys their presence, though invisible, blanketing our earth. Further, Scripture affirms, "The angel of the Lord encamps all around those who fear Him, and delivers them" (Psalm 34:7).

Jesus referred to these angel companions. "Take heed that you do not despise one of these little ones, for I say to you that in heaven their angels always see the face of My Father who is in heaven" (Matthew 18: 10). Numerous stories, Biblical and otherwise, confirm the presence in our world of an invisible army of beings called angels. One released Peter from prison; another ministered to Jesus in the wilderness of temptation and in Gethsemane. One rolled away the stone from Christ's tomb and called Him forth to life.

Clearly, the Bible depicts our world as a danger zone dependent upon the protecting and ever watchful presence of holy angels. If our eyes could be opened and we behold the multitude of dangers threatening on every side day and night, we would have a greater sensibility of our debt to God and holy angels for every moment of comfort and joy that we know.

Revelation 7 repeats the prophecy of Zechariah 6, confirming the protecting ministry of angels in our world and expanding their job description to include—destruction.

---

[13] "Spirit" has several meanings in Scripture.

After these things I saw four angels standing at the four corners of the earth, holding the four winds of the earth, that the wind should not blow on the earth, on the sea, or on any tree. Then I saw another angel ascending from the east, having the seal of the living God. And He cried with a loud voice to the four angels to whom it was granted to harm the earth and the sea, saying do not harm the earth, the sea or the trees till we have sealed the servants of our God on their foreheads" (v. 1-3).

Again, we note four angels positioned at the four points of the compass, signifying their presence everywhere in our world. The Bible often uses the symbol of "winds" to denote strife among men and nations (Daniel 7: 2; Jeremiah 25:31,32;49:36,37). These mighty angels, in response to orders from the heavenly command center to "Hold," restrain the winds of strife among nations from blowing upon the earth.

Note especially that to these "angels of mercy" is granted power to harm earth and sea. How will they do it? By picking up weapons and going forth to slay? or by ceasing to protect? Need they do more than release, withdraw, back off from their protecting duties to allow death and utter chaos into the social order?

Since these angels take directions from God, and Christ represented God, we may assume that heavenly angels behave as Christ behaved under similar circumstances.

Neither God nor holy angels abandon their protecting duties until thoroughly discharged by their beneficiaries, who, self-sufficient, have never learned their utter dependence upon a power outside themselves, never dreamed that a compassionate Providence undergirded all their earthly triumphs. In attitude they say, as Judah said anciently of Christ, "We will not have this Man to reign over us" (Luke 19:14), never considering that when He goes, *His protection goes with Him.*

The Holy Spirit

A second way in which God sustains His creation is through the living presence of the Holy Spirit in our world. Scripture abounds in evidence of this. As far back as the exodus, He said, "I will set My tabernacle among you, and My soul shall not abhor you. I will walk among you and be your God, and you shall be My people" (Leviticus 26:11, 12). The earthly tabernacle itself, first erected in the wilderness, later at Shiloh and then Jerusalem, represented God's presence with His people, a predominate Scriptural theme (See Exodus 25:8).

Many were the symbols through which God sought to teach His people this vital truth. "As the mountains surround Jerusalem, so the Lord surrounds His people" (Psalm 125:2). "You have hedged me behind and before" (Psalm

139:5). "The reproaches of those who reproach You have fallen on me" (Psalm 69:9). The last, a prophecy of Christ, also applies to individuals living in God the Holy Spirit, as He did.

Not only does this picture convey God's ideal for abiding with His people, it describes His plan for protecting them as well. "You have been a shelter for me, and a strong tower from the enemy. I will abide in Your tabernacle forever; I will trust in the shelter of Your wings"; "He who dwells in the secret place of the Most High shall abide under the shadow of the Almighty. . . . He shall cover you with His feathers, and under His wings you shall take refuge" (Psalm 61:3,4; 91:1,4). Again we note a picture of the Scriptural "faith of Jesus" (Galatians 2:16; Revelation 14:12), the most mentioned theme of God's word.

Nothing is clearer in Scripture than God's plan to live in His people through the Holy Spirit, nor more certain than human dependence upon this connection for salvation and protection. "With favor You will surround Him as with a shield" (Psalm 5:12). This concept appears perhaps clearest in (but is not limited to) the book of Psalms and the writings of the apostle Paul. Nature itself depends upon this heavenly ministry to maintain order, generate life, and assure the predictability so essential to the security of life on our planet. As long as God's Spirit and holy angels remain, life continues in familiar patterns. What could ever cause them to depart?

The Devil is Real

Into this harmonious scene, enter the villain.

"So the great dragon was cast out, that serpent of old, called the Devil and Satan, who deceives the whole world; he was cast to the earth, and his angels were cast out with him" (Revelation 12:9).

Considering the size of the Bible, it is significant that it gives relatively little direct attention to the devil. Because God is a positive Being, He gives this negative creature as little notice as possible, consistent with the need to warn against him. However, enough information exists to reveal who he is and what he does. Revelation 12, Ezekiel 28 and Isaiah 14, plus brief statements here and there constitute the body of explicit Scriptural data regarding him. In brief, here is the story it tells.

In heaven's atmosphere all the lines flow outward. *Agape*, that special kind of other-centered love, permeates the air and governs every relationship and transaction. Besides the Father, Son, Holy Spirit and holy angels, a beautiful angel lived there whose name was Lucifer. He was the "covering angel" before God's throne, leader of the celestial choir, a being of unsurpassed beauty among the creation of God (Ezekiel 28:13, 14; Psalm 99:1).

As long as the lines of other-centeredness flowed outward, there was peace and harmony and order among the inhabitants. But somehow Lucifer began to look at himself instead of looking at God. He saw he was beautiful, wise and adored by the other angels. Gradually his lines began to bend and turn around, and finally, all Lucifer could see was himself. He thought that an angel as beautiful and wise as he, adored by the other angels, should be "like the Most High," that he should be worshiped as God. Toward this end Lucifer gave his powers, deceiving the angels who loved him and causing them to feel that God was unjust in depriving him of worship. When at last rebellion erupted, one-third of the angels aligned themselves with him in revolt against their Maker.

Having exhausted his welcome in heaven, he drew the first family of earth into his camp and set up headquarters here. Although earth's parents, like heavenly beings, were created with lines flowing outward, in yielding to this rebel, their lines turned inward like his own. Their nature changed. Created to seek the good of others, they now more easily sought their own good.[14] And in the heavens the universe watched to see what would happen to a world where all the lines flow in.

But first certain issues must be settled. How deep is God's love for His creatures? Could anything be salvaged from this lost planet? Could fallen humans receive God's love and reflect it in their world? God answered with the cross, the ultimate expression of both His justice and His love. And while the world learns what really happened there, accepts it or rejects it, His angels hold the winds, thus "capping" sin's natural effects. But when, in response to human free will, God gives the command, "Release," the universe will see how fast sin self-destructs.

---

[14]God's sense of responsibility appears most striking in contrast with the character of Satan, whom Scripture terms, among other thing, "the accuser" (Revelation 12:10). Adam's fall in Eden reveals both masters.

Satan deceived Eve into the forbidden act, but Adam was not deceived (1 Timothy 2:14). He knew his beloved companion must die for her transgression, and he determined to die with her. Notice how his love for her at this point faintly reflects the love of God for a fallen human race.

When Adam fell, the quality of his love for Eve instantly changed to reflect that of his new master. "The woman whom You gave to be with me, she gave me of the tree, and I ate," he said (Genesis 3:12). It was the woman's fault, You see. Or perhaps, God, it was Your fault for giving me this defective woman. It was someone, anyone else's fault but, certainly, not mine.

This accusing nature got into the gene pool and passed to the entire human race. For this reason, God calls for repentance as the first step back to His kingdom. Humans cannot see their sin and accept the blame apart from the deep moving of the Holy Spirit on their heart, for it violates their nature. Thus God looks for repentance as the first sign of eternal life aborning in the soul.

The Destroyer

The Bible clearly depicts Lucifer, whose name was changed to Satan, as a liar and deceiver. It also denotes him as the destroyer, a point vital to the present study.

Scripture frequently mentions the destroyer, but in order to verify his identity, we must begin with Revelation 9:1, 11. "I saw a star fallen from heaven to the earth. And to him was given the key to the bottomless pit": "And they [the "locusts"] had as king over them the angel of the bottomless pit, whose name in Hebrew is *Abaddon*, but in Greek he has the name *Apollyon*."

(Symbolically, the terms "angel" 'and "star" can be interchangeable. See Revelation 12, especially verses 4 and 9.)

Both names, *Abaddon* and *Apollyon*, mean "destroyer." The following parallel texts clearly identify this "fallen star."

- How are you fallen from heaven, O Lucifer, son of the morning. . . . Yet you shall be brought down to Sheol, to the lowest depths of the pit (Isaiah 14:12, 15).

- I saw Satan fall like lightning from heaven (Luke 10:18).

- So the great dragon was cast out [of heaven], that serpent of old, called the devil and Satan . . . he was cast to the earth (Revelation 12:9).

Isaiah 14 adds: You "made the world as a wilderness and destroyed its cities," destroyed the land and slew the people. Close comparison of Revelation 9 with Isaiah 14:12-20 and Revelation 12 leaves no question that the "destroyer" of Revelation 9:12 is Satan himself. Do we have to ask why God finds it necessary to shelter us against this death machine?

In some familiar statements of Scripture, God says, "My Spirit shall not always strive with man," and "grieve not the Spirit" (Genesis 6:3; Ephesians 4:30). King David, following his dual sin of adultery and murder, prayed, "Do not take Your Holy Spirit from me" (Psalm 51:7). What determines whether God and His angel representatives "stay" or "leave"? That is the pivotal question of our study.

Obedience Gives Authority

"Know ye not, that to whom ye yield yourselves servants to obey, his servants ye are to whom ye obey: whether of sin unto death, or of obedience unto righteousness?" (Romans 6:16, KJV).

In response to the charges and claims of Satan and in harmony with His commitment to our free will, God has agreed to let humans make their own decision as to who will be their master. Since our lines naturally flow inward, we are by nature children of "wrath," as the Bible calls it (Ephesians 2:3). Satan has us by default. God countered with the cross.

When a person or a people refuse irreversibly to surrender to the claims of the cross, when their lives show deliberate indifference to God's expressed will, Satan declares himself victor. According to the terms of the great conflict between God and Satan, God must leave the field. The people have cast Him off. When their free-will decisions are final and the gentle wooing of His Spirit no longer moves them, then they have given themselves over to the kingdom of darkness, and Satan stakes a claim on their souls.

The Possible Meaning of Disasters

Though I'm not a prophet nor the child of one I do confess to speculating occasionally on how this picture might fit events occurring in the visible world today. In that connection, on October 10, 1986 the [Boise] *Idaho Statesman* newspaper published an article on the nuclear production reactor at Hanford, Washington, stating, "At 5:30 a.m. a highly concentrated plutonium solution was transferred from one holding tank to another. . . . Only after the transfer had been made did someone realize that a pipe linking the second tank to a third tank was still connected. If the concentrated plutonium solution had entered the third tank, the liquid could have gone 'critical,' the point at which a nuclear chain reaction takes place. . . . A series of six valves that had remained closed throughout the incident prevented the transfer of liquid. Still the episode—one of 54 'criticality' incidents at Hanford in the last two years—was so disturbing that the U.S. Department of Energy took the unprecedented step October 8 of indefinitely shutting down the plant." Except for site cleanup, it is still closed over a decade later with no plans to reopen.

Did an angel hand secure those six valves? What could happen to such valves if God loses authority over them in deference to human free will?

Global warming cannot fully explain the increase in the number and strength of natural disasters occurring around us today. The world trembles at the ferocity of tornadoes and hurricanes, which slam coastline cities, killing thousands and leaving hundreds of thousands homeless and destitute. Volcanoes, dormant for centuries, awaken, their fire and brimstone breath threatening communities which have for generations lived peacefully on their fertile slopes.

The thought of invisible intelligences monitoring earth life may sound like the figment of a screenwriter's imagination, but scientific insights do not rule it out.

Lincoln Barnett, in *The Universe and Dr. Einstein*, points out a fact well known both in and out of the world of science, that human sensory equipment cannot begin to register all that takes place around us in our world. Referring only to the sense of sight, he says, "The human eye fails to respond to most of the 'lights' in the world and . . . what man can perceive of the reality around him is distorted and enfeebled by the limitations of his organ of vision. The world would appear far different to him if his eye were sensitive, for example, to x-rays" [2d ed. (Harper & Brothers, 1957), p. 13].

In response to the question of what is "real" in our world, he says, "It is as though the true objective world lies forever half concealed beneath a translucent, plastic dome. Peering through its cloudy surface, deformed and distorted by the ever-changing perspectives of theory, man faintly espies certain apparently stable relationships and recurring events. A consistent isomorphic representation of these relationships and events is the maximal possibility of his knowledge. Beyond that point he stares into the void" (*ibid.*, pp. 114-15).

Knowing how little we know makes more plausible that invisible world of which we are told, occupied by demons and holy angels, whispered temptations and promptings to holiness, that world where the Holy Spirit in the persona of Christ walks and talks with the blessed.

Our world, so immediate and palpable to us, holds a dimension of reality into which our senses cannot penetrate. A higher level of intelligences watch our world, watch the contest between moral soundness and perversity. In this vast theater one absolute rule prevails: Humans get the master they choose to obey. They cannot manipulate another outcome. Neither side will forfeit anyone.

How Does God Destroy?

The two powers in charge of the contest possess opposite characters. With One, the lines flow out. His word reveals Him as totally other-centered, totally supportive, totally creative, redemptive, healing. The other is described as the destroyer, his whole purpose being to deceive and thereby to destroy. No one ever argues that Satan redeems. Yet it has often appeared to us as if God destroys! But those who are wise, who see the problems with the traditional view of a destroying God, will ask the question: *How does He do it?*

The Bible invariably describes God's destructive acts in terms amenable to human perception. But we have noted the inadequacy of human senses to pick up the whole picture.

The Biblical story of the plagues of Egypt suggests a deeper level of destructive activity than appears visually. Designed to induce Pharaoh to free the Hebrew slaves, the plagues afford another of those puzzling apparent contradictions of Scripture. You will recall (Exodus 1-13) they consisted of waters turned to blood, frogs in the land, lice in the land, flies in the land, diseased livestock, boils on man and beast, hail, locusts, and finally death of the firstborn. In each case the language suggests that God, by a specific act, brought these disasters down upon the heads of the hapless Egyptians.

God speaks. "'For I will pass through the land of Egypt on that night, and will strike all the firstborn in the land of Egypt, both man and beast; and against all the gods of Egypt I will execute judgment: I am the Lord'" (Exodus 12:12).

The surface message here suggests that since the Egyptians' sinfulness had gone too far, God personally executed their firstborn in order to persuade Pharaoh to release the Hebrews from slavery.

But the Bible contains some specific references to the plagues which intimate something very different occurring beyond human vision than we note in the surface view:

Who Killed the Firstborn of Egypt?

One Perspective	Another Perspective
God speaking: "For *I* will pass through the land of Egypt on that night and will strike all the firstborn in the land of Egypt, both man and beast; against all the gods of Egypt *I will execute judgment*: I am the Lord" (Exodus 12:12).	For the Lord will pass through to strike the Egyptians: and when He sees the blood on the doorposts, the Lord will pass over the door and not allow *the destroyer* to come into your houses to strike you (Exodus 12:23)

Note verse 23 carefully. It suggests two actors in that terrible drama: "The Lord" and "the [definite article] destroyer." If the Lord does not see the blood, he will come down. Why? To strike (as we would express it)? No. To "allow" the destroyer to strike.

An Illustration

Regarding this, the final Egyptian plague, God gave careful instructions that only homes with the blood of an animal sprinkled on their doorposts, representing faith in the death of Christ yet future, would escape the terrible curse. Let us then picture two homes standing side by side on that night, one with the blood, one without.

The midnight hour arrives. Invisibly God's "death angel" appears, carrying in its hands the destroying weapon from the eternal Throne. He looks at one house, sees the blood and passes over. He sees no blood on the house next door, and he comes down. What does he carry in his hand? Is that a sword? Perhaps a laser or a lightning bolt? No. It is a document on which is stamped the name of God. He shows it to the guardian angel, throughout the years stationed at the door of the house devoid of the saving blood. "Release," says the document. Together the angels fly away, exposing the firstborn within to the destroyer, waiting eagerly without.

The next chapter looks at what limits the destroyer to the firstborn. Notice that this perspective agrees with the way in which God dealt with sin in the case of Christ the Sin Bearer.

What Was the Father's Role In the Death of Jesus?

One Perspective	Another Perspective
I [God] will strike the Shepherd. . . . We esteemed Him stricken, *smitten by God* (Mark 14: 27; Isaiah 53:4).	My God, My God, why have You *forsaken* Me?(Mark 15:34).

In each case God backs off, releasing entrenched sin into the power of the destroyer. In each case He sees and describes Himself as "striking" or doing what He only allows.

The book of Psalms has a final word to say regarding this terrible experience, faintly underscoring our new model of the episode and calling into question our traditional picture of God's participation in it:

> He cast on them the fierceness of His *anger*,
>> *Wrath, indignation,* and *trouble*,
>>> By sending angels of destruction among them.
>>> He made a path for His anger;
>> He did not spare their soul from death,
>>> But *gave their life over* to the plague,
>>>> And destroyed all the firstborn in Egypt.
>>>> (Psalm 78:46, 48-50, 60-62)

As Christ was *delivered up*, so Egypt was *given over* to destruction.

The evidence mounts that God destroys in a way very different from the way in which Satan or humans destroy. It suggests He withdraws—simply and reluctantly—leaving off His protecting duties in compliance with human free moral choice.

God expressed His "anger, wrath, indignation, and trouble" through the plagues, including destruction of the firstborn. In the next chapter we shall examine a previously overlooked Biblical definition of these terms, which supports our alternate model.

THE JOB SYNDROME

"Shall we indeed accept good from God,
and shall we not accept adversity?
In all this Job did not sin with his lips" (Job 2:10).

"There was a man in the land of Uz whose name was Job; that man was blameless and upright, one who feared God and shunned evil" (Job 1:1).

Thus begins a book traditionally held to be the first written of those collected in the Holy Bible. Whether the tradition is true or not, it seems fitting that it should be, because the book of Job deals with the oldest questions of all: Why? What is God's role and purpose in human suffering? Why do the righteous suffer? Humans have asked these questions since the beginning; how like God to have answered them long ago in the book of Job!

Here Satan presents himself before the heavenly council as representative of earth. He and God exchange comments regarding one Job of Uz. God says, "So, you say humans cannot avoid sin? Have you noticed my righteous servant Job?"

Satan: Yes, but you've hedged him around with angels. He obeys you for the goodies. Just let me at him; he'll blame You and curse You to Your face.

God: You're wrong, Satan. Job serves Me because he knows and loves Me.

They agree to a contest. Poor Job! All he can see are his children and livestock destroyed, his body a mass of loathsome sores. He sees no more than we ordinarily see, when we read Scriptural accounts of destructive acts attributed to God. Job's senses cannot penetrate into the invisible world. But in this instance we have an advantage over Job. We can see. We have what writers call the "omniscient" viewpoint. This once in Scripture the curtain draws aside, revealing the actors within the invisible world itself; we know Why, and we know How.

The remaining chapters find the protagonist tragically reduced in fortune and engaged in philosophical debate with some so-called friends, trying to make sense of this disaster.

In response to his friends' insistence that God blesses the righteous, Job says, "Who does not know such things as these? . . . I know it is so. . . . What you know I also know; I am not inferior to you" (Job 11:3; 9:2; 13:2). He seems to have agreed rather than disagreed with his friends on the basic rule that God blesses His own.

If Job believed as his friends believed, interpreting prosperity as a signal of God's favor, in what respect was he right and they wrong, as the book's ending clearly shows? Job says, "God has *delivered me* to the ungodly, and *turned me over* to the hands of the wicked" (Job 16:11). Job's friends seemed not to understand the exception that proves the rule: Sometimes for a redemptive purpose God temporarily and in a limited way exposes His own to trouble, a situation I call "the Job Syndrome." Job, knowing himself, was perhaps in a better position than they to see this truth.

The Wrath of God

While Job seemed to understand the dynamics of "the wrath of God," Christians have generally viewed it as a blow God personally administers when He gets mad. He's been patient ever so long; humans have spurned His grace. He can't reach them any more. We have tied logic in knots, trying to explain how a God who never stops loving, whose lines never stop flowing outward to meet His creatures' needs, can also be a God who rains fire, drops humans into cracks in the earth, drowns them! Job seemed to understand there is more to the "wrath of God" than meets the eye.

Here as in so many cases of heavenly truth, we must be open to reversing our traditional understanding. When we allow the Bible to explain itself, we find that the wrath of God is another of the apparent paradoxes of Scripture and the diametric opposite of our usual way of thinking. The following references reveal that the wrath (indignation or fury or anger) of God occurs when He withdraws from a person or people because they have made a final decision to continue in a course of willful sin, thus depriving Him of authority to involve Himself in their affairs. God's absence leaves that person or people vulnerable to the destroyer. While numerous references in virtually all books of the Bible support this position, most of them contain only two or three elements of the formula. The following references contain all four.

FORMULA CODE	
[Because sin is chosen]	*Results in trouble*
God withdraws	/Equals His wrath/

- "My /anger/ shall be aroused against them in that day, and I will **forsake** them, and I will **hide My face** from them, and they shall be *devoured*. And many *evils and troubles* shall befall them, so that they will say in that day, 'Have not these *evils* come upon us because our **God is not among us**?' And I will surely **hide My face** in that day because of all the [evil] which they have done, in that [they have turned to other gods]" (Deuteronomy 31:17, 18).

- "I will *slay* in My /anger/ and My /fury/ all for whose [wickedness] I have **hidden My face** from this city" (Jeremiah 33:5).

- "For our fathers have [trespassed] and done [evil] in the eyes of the Lord our God . . . Therefore the /wrath/ of the Lord fell upon Judah and Jerusalem, and he has **given them up** to *trouble* . . . " (2 Chronicles 29:6, 8).

- [They caused their sons and daughters to pass through the fire, practiced witchcraft and soothsaying, and sold themselves to do evil] in the sight of the Lord, to provoke Him to /anger/. Therefore, the Lord was very /angry/ with Israel, and **removed them from His sight**. . . . The Lord **rejected** all the descendants of Israel, *afflicted* them, and **delivered them into the hand of plunderers**, until He had **cast them from His sight** (2 Kings 17:17-20).

- "For the [iniquity of his covetousness] I was /angry/ and *struck* him; **I hid** and was /angry/" (Isaiah 57:17).

The Bible speaks of the "defiling" of the earth itself. (See, for example, Isaiah 24:5; Psalm 106:38; Deuteronomy 35:33.) Could this refer to God's losing authority over a specific geographic location in deference to the choice of humans residing there to separate from Him through sin?

God lets us choose His kingdom or ours. He will respect that choice. We are accountable for what we know and what we *can* know, if we will open our eyes and look (John 9:41).When humans spurn God's grace irretrievably, Satan stakes a claim on their soul. If we have failed in our lives to provide God with arguments against Satan's claims, if our lives show no genuine commitment to the principles of heaven, what can God do? What can He say? Since God sees our vulnerability apart from His loving omnipotence, in the most emphatic language at times, He says He *does* what human free will has deprived Him of authority to *prevent*. All He has really done, all He can do, is walk away, acknowledging that the human decision is final.

Note that in Scriptural accounts of destructive acts attributed to God, we "see" only the results; we do not "see" the means. Therefore, patterning God after ourselves (Psalm 50:21), we have assumed He destroys as we would destroy. But might not our God, knowing He has *the power to prevent* a disaster, feel the same burden of responsibility as if He had administered the blow Himself? In the language of Scripture He takes the blame, as He took the blame on Calvary so long ago. Satan is the accuser; God, by contrast, has always said, Let the blame fall on Me.

But what of Job? He certainly had not rejected God out of his life. Job can be viewed as a symbol of Christ, a righteous man whom God treated as a sinner in order to fulfill a necessary, redemptive purpose. God honored Job in allowing this patient man to vindicate Him against the challenge of the prince of darkness—to demonstrate that his loyalty to God had nothing to do with his fortunes—a purpose which Job would likely have approved had he known. And passing through the sorrow, Job ultimately realized the fulfillment of the good promises of God in his life (see Job 42:12), as Jesus did in His, for Scripture says of Christ, "God also has highly exalted Him and given Him the name which is above every name, that at the name of Jesus every knee should bow, . . . " and "every tongue . . . confess that Jesus Christ is Lord" (Philippians 2:9, 10).

Principles of Living

Consideration of the reasons for suffering would be incomplete without mentioning the role of law in human fortune. Penalties exist for law breaking, and laws exist governing our health, our interpersonal relationships, our finances. When we break the laws or principles by which these systems operate, we may suffer the results of disobedience. It is most unkind and inaccurate to blame God for our suffering in cases such as these. In fact, I suspect we might be surprised if we knew how often God has shielded us from the results of our own folly and transgressions. But can we expect Him to continue this, once we clearly understand the issues?

Now let us compare the message of Job with our deeper insights into God's character.

- Satan, the destroyer, is the executor of human suffering.

- When entrenched sin deprives God of authority to shield, He has no option but to release the protecting "hedge" (Job 1:10).

- God sets the boundaries for Satan's destructive work (Job 1:12; 2:6).

  He did in limiting him to Job's possessions first and then to his body, sparing Job's life. He did in limiting the destroyer to the lice, frogs, etc., and to Egypt's firstborn. At world's end, however, His judgments will fall "without mixture" or dilution with mercy, or limit (Revelation 14:10, KJV).

- God takes the blame. He sees and describes Himself as doing what He does not prevent.

In this connection, here is more data for our familiar chart:

Who Assaulted Job?

One Perspective	Another Perspective
Satan says: "Stretch out *Your* hand and touch all that he has, and he will surely curse You to Your face!" (Job 1:11). After Satan's first assault against Job, God said to Satan, "You incited *Me* against him to destroy him without cause (Job 2:3).	"Behold, all that he has is in *your [Satan's]* power (Job 1:12).

Here we catch God in the very act of accepting blame for destruction He only allowed. Comparing this with the loss of Egypt's firstborn, we have. . . .

Who Killed the Firstborn of Egypt?

One Perspective	Another Perspective
God speaking: "For *I* will pass through the land of Egypt on that night and will strike all the firstborn in the land of Egypt, both man and beast; against all the gods of Egypt *I* will execute judgment: I am the Lord" (Exodus 12:12).	For the Lord will pass through to strike the Egyptians: and when He sees the blood on the doorposts, the Lord will pass over the door and not allow *the destroyer* to come into your houses to strike you (Exodus 12:2).

. . . and with the death of Christ:

What Was the Father's Role In the Death of Jesus?

One Perspective	Another Perspective
I [God] will strike the Shepherd. . . . We esteemed Him stricken, *smitten by God* (Mark 14: 27; Isaiah 53:4)	My God, My God, why have You *forsaken* Me?(Mark 15:34).

Insights from Job fully support the idea that God does not destroy as humans destroy. Rather, He withdraws His protection, releasing humans to whatever fate may await them outside Himself. But *He sees and describes Himself as doing what He only permits*, thus validating our hypothesis. The book of Job reveals a world usually closed to human vision. Other examples of God's wrath limit us to sensory evidence. Does the traditional picture based on sensory descriptions give the full account? Or does the story of Job contain principles applying not just to a single event of antiquity but to human adversity throughout time?

| 6 | **SOME FATAL EXAMPLES** |

*"He that loveth not
knoweth not God,
for God is love" (1 John 4:8, KJV)*

By now you may be looking at such statements as the following with new eyes:

> See, Lord and consider! To whom have You done this? Should the women eat their offspring, the children they have cuddled? Should the priest and prophet be slain in the sanctuary of the Lord? . . . You have slaughtered and not pitied. You have invited as to a feast day the terrors that surround me. In the day of *the Lord's anger* there was no refugee or survivor(Lamentations 2:20-22).

You now have the tools to review some classic Bible descriptions of God's wrath and see things you may not have seen before. Here are some "favorites":

- "Uzza put out his hand to hold the ark . . . Then the *anger of the Lord* was aroused against Uzza, and He *struck* him because he put his hand to the ark, and he died there before God(1 Chronicles 13:9, 10).

- That same night the angel of Yahweh went out and *struck* down a hundred and eighty-five thousand men in the Assyrian camp(Isaiah 37:36; 2 Kings 19:35, JB).

- While the meat was still between their teeth . . . the *wrath of the Lord* was aroused against the people, and the Lord *struck* the people with a very great plague. . . . There they buried the people who had yielded to craving(Numbers 11:33, 34).

- Then Ananias . . . fell down and breathed his last. . . . Then immediately she [Sapphira] fell down . . . and breathed her last(Acts 5:5, 10).

If God's wrath in other places is His removing Himself from the arena of willful, entrenched sin, why isn't it here?

If God's striking the firstborn of Egypt, the patriarch Job, and His own Son entailed releasing them to the power of the destroyer, why isn't it the same here? and other places as well? Would not the results—perceivable evidence—be the same? If you cannot agree that God's role in all these incidents is consistent and in harmony with His changelessness (See Malachi 3:6), you assume the burden of proving it is not.

Further, note what took place when God struck Miriam with leprosy:

> So the *anger of the Lord* was aroused against them, and *He departed.* And when the cloud departed from above the tabernacle, suddenly Miriam became leprous, as white as snow(Numbers 12:9, 10).

What did God do when he became angry? He departed. Only then did Miriam appear leprous.

Shiloh

Another revealing incident surrounds loss of Israel's first religious center at Shiloh. Eli, the High Priest, did not control his sons, also priests, and their wayward example led Israel into spiritual decline. Their influence weakened national defenses to the extent they suffered a great military defeat by the Philistines. Then someone got a "great" idea.

Let's bring the ark of the covenant out to war with us. It will bring victory. They had begun to view the ark as a god in itself, rather than as a visual aid to draw their minds toward the invisible Creator. When the ark entered Israel's camp, a great triumphant shout rose from the soldiers. The Philistines, good scouts that they were, noted the whole thing and trembled, for they too viewed the ark as Israel's god, and a mighty one at that. They concluded, if they were going down, to fight like warriors and make a battle of it.

But to everyone's surprise, Philistia included, Israel suffered an overwhelming defeat that day. And, worst of all, the Philistines captured the ark of God.

A runner brought news of the disaster to Eli at Shiloh, whereupon the old man fell backward in his chair and died. His daughter-in-law chose this ignoble moment to give birth to a son, whom she named Ichabod, *"The glory has departed."*

In a series of little-noticed Bible references, God gives another history of Shiloh—the invisible history, describing Shiloh's fate in terms particularly relevant to ancient Israel.

Anyone remotely familiar with Old Testament history knows the pathos with which God called upon that nation to repent in order to avoid a disastrous end. With every tool of persuasion available to him, God urged Israel to change directions. One illustration he used was the fate of Shiloh. "I will treat this temple as I treated Shiloh," He said of Jerusalem. "This temple shall be like Shiloh." Just go to Shiloh; see how desolate and uninhabited it is. I shall treat this place, Jerusalem, the hub of religious life in Israel, exactly as I treated her (Jeremiah 7:12; 26:9).

But what actually happened there? The Psalmist describes, in the invisible world at Shiloh, events that brought desolation upon that city:

> When God heard this, He was furious,
> And greatly abhorred Israel,
> So that *He forsook the tabernacle of Shiloh,*
> The tent which He had placed among men.
> (Psalm 78:59, 60)

The people of Shiloh committed themselves irretrievably to ignore God's commands, and then the glory departed, exposing Israel to defeat before her enemies. The years rolled by and eventually Jerusalem itself fell by the same dynamics (See Chapter 7).

The Demoniacs of Gadara

Another interesting illustration of God's role in destruction occurs in the gospel story of the demoniacs of Gadara. When Jesus cast a legion of evil spirits out of these men (one version indicates only one madman), the demons *requested permission* to enter some nearby swine. In a move perhaps designed to reveal the hearts of local residents, permission was granted. Only then could the demons destroy, as they panicked the swine and plunged them over a cliff. (See Mark 5, Matthew 8, Luke 8.).

Here Deity only *allowed* a destructive act. The demons could not act out their destructive purposes without that permission. The attitude of local residents in response to this episode reflects economic rather than human concerns. The herdsmen of Gadara might have rejoiced at the deliverance of these unfortunate men, but they did not. Instead, responding to what they perceived as an economic threat, they put the blame on Jesus and cast their Savior out.

Phrases To Watch For

As a prelude to consideration of some of the "weightier" Biblical stories of God's seeming dark side, some attention must be focused on meaningful recurring phrases relating to this issue.

You will recall that Jesus, in the persona of sin, was "delivered up" for destruction. Some Bible translations say "handed over" rather than "delivered up." These and other phrases occur regularly in Scripture in connection with statements of God's "wrath" or "anger." Watch for them. You may wish to begin your investigation with the book of Psalms, in which this relationship particularly stands out. (See also Judges; 2 Chronicles 12-36.) Other phrases to watch for are "gave him/them over," "abandoned," "forsook/forsaken," "rejected," or that God "hid His face."

Once you begin noticing them, you will find them everywhere in Scripture, connected with those passages dealing with God's wrath.[15]

Testimony of the Apostle Paul

The writings of the apostle Paul, as well, hold some intriguing information on this topic.[16] Some of his comments not only add to our understanding of the dynamics of "wrath," but also seem to *broaden the scope of the spiritual authority of the church* in this arena.

He specifically identifies the destiny of one who is "handed over" or "delivered up." He directs the church to "deliver such a [licentious] one to Satan for the destruction of the flesh" (1 Corinthians 5:4, 5).[17] He also states that he himself "delivered [Hymenaeus and Alexander] to Satan" (1 Timothy 1:20).[18] Satan may personally administer such destruction, or it may come from natural disasters awaiting God's release to occur in a local area. Either way, Satan triumphs in the death of the unsaved.

---

[15]Obviously, the fact that God "delivered" Daniel from the lions' den has a very different connotation from what we are discussing here.

[16]Chapter 7 will include a discussion of Paul's comments in Romans 1, a clear statement on the wrath of God.

[17]Note Paul's motive here: That the flesh, the carnal mind, might be destroyed. As in the gradual abandonment of Pharoah's Egypt God desired to instruct and save that nation, so Paul desires the "handing over" to overrule Satan's purpose by bringing those so abandoned to repentance and change of heart.

[18]Paul states he handed these two individuals over to Satan in order that they learn not to blaspheme. Hymenaeus, it seems, along with Philetus, was teaching the false doctrine that the resurrection had already taken place.   *(Continued next page)*

The "Dark Side" of God

The point is, when humans choose to ignore God to the extent they will *never* change their minds, never love the great Lover of our race, He will not—because He cannot—inflict Himself upon them unwanted.

A typical statement covering this dynamic occurs in 2 Chronicles 15:2: "The Lord is with you while you are with Him. If you seek Him, He will be found by you; but if you forsake Him, He will forsake you." The choice for separation is always, first, a human decision. But given this human decision, God has no choice but to honor it. "My people would not heed My voice, and Israel would have none of Me. So *I gave them over* to their own stubborn heart, to walk in their own counsels." Rather than feeling glee at His chance now to "get them" for their rebellion, He says, "Oh, that My people would listen to Me, that Israel would walk in My ways! I would soon subdue their enemies, and turn My hand against their adversaries" (Psalm 81:11-14). No joy here in human waywardness. Such is the "dark side" of God.

Continued from previous page

Alexander the coppersmith had done Paul unspecified "great harm" in opposing his message, insomuch that Paul had to call upon God for rescue "from the lion's mouth." The apostle is not inclined to be charitable regarding Alexander, for he calls upon the Lord to reward him for his deed. See 2 Timothy 2:17, 18; 4:14-17. These men challenged and mocked God in a work He had undertaken. This Paul calls blasphemy and deems suitable grounds for exercising his spiritual authority and releasing them, in the name of Jesus, into the hands of Satan. Note especially, Paul made no move to harm these men himself nor to incite others to harm them. He relied solely on the principles of divine abandonment.

7

*"Ye know not what manner
of spirit ye are of" (Luke.9:55, KJV).*

"Then the Lord rained brimstone and fire on Sodom and Gomorrah,
from the Lord out of the heavens. So He overthrew those cities, all the plain,
all the inhabitants of the cities, and what grew on the ground. But his [Lot's]
wife looked back behind him, and she became a pillar of salt" (Genesis 19:24-
26).

Enough has been said by now that students of this topic can draw
their own conclusions as to the way in which God destroyed Sodom and
Gomorrah. However, some specific Biblical evidence exists regarding those
cities, which supports our present thesis.

Until recently no information existed outside Scripture regarding the five
Cities of the Plain involved in the story we call "Sodom and Gomorrah."
For this reason many scholars questioned the story's authenticity, attributing
it to Middle Eastern folklore. Those few who thought it might have some
historical basis expected to find archeological evidence of this beneath the
shallow southern end of the Dead Sea, basing their belief on the Scriptural
description of the area as "the Valley of Siddim (that is, the Salt Sea)"
(Genesis 14:3). Israelis call the Dead Sea *Yam Hamaelach*, Salt Sea, to this
day.

In the late 1970s, however, the lowering of the Dead Sea's water level
allowed excavation extensive enough to shatter this hope, since no trace of
these or any cities could be found.

Meantime, some interesting things were happening in the area
immediately east of the southern end of the Dead Sea. As early as 1924 the
noted scholar, William Foxwell Albright, and M. G. Kyle, president of Xenia
Theological Seminary, excavated an elaborate place of worship there, which
they termed Bab edh-Dhra. The site received little attention until 1973,
when other archaeologists discovered in the same area ruins of an ancient
city, which they called Numeira. Interestingly, Numeira showed clear surface
evidence of having been burned.

Although work continues, archeologists now state that this area contains he ruins of exactly five cities, no more, no less, and that several display spongy char," the residue of burning, so profusely one may scoop it up with he hand.

Sodom and Gomorrah Found?

Scripture describes the cities' location on the plain of Jordan as "well watered . . . like the Garden of the Lord, like the land of Egypt as you go toward Zoar" (Genesis 13:10). You will remember that God spared the small city of Zoar at Lot's request that he be given asylum there.

Seeing this area today, one can scarcely believe it was ever so productive. Now a virtual wasteland, it fights the indigenous people who seek to wrest a livelihood from it. The writer of Genesis suggests that even in his time the land had changed dramatically, for in portraying the former productivity of his area, he says this was "before the Lord destroyed Sodom and Gomorrah" Genesis 13:10). That terrible event apparently changed the character of the and down to our own time.

In contrast with the barrenness surrounding these sites, the countless streams feeding into the southeastern Dead Sea make the shoreline still very fertile, hinting that the rest of the land could have been equally productive at some time in the ancient past.

In 1980 the prestigious journal *Biblical Archeology Review* reported that Walter E. Rast of Valparaiso University, Valparaiso, Indiana, and R. Thomas Schaub of Indiana University of Pennsylvania, who were then excavating these five ruins, believed they had found the ancient Cities of the Plain. "Have Sodom and Gomorrah Been Found?," September/October, pp. 27-36; 300 Connecticut Avenue NW, Suite 300, Washington, D.C. 20008).

Scripture further describes this area anciently: "Now the Valley of Siddim was full of asphalt ['bitumen,' RSV] pits" (Genesis 14:10), suggesting some type of igneous activity occurring within the earth's crust. Today "the shores around the Dead Sea are covered with lava, sulfur, and rock salt. Gases escape from the surface of the water" (*World Book Encyclopedia*, 1954, Vol. 4, p. 1891). Note the existence in this scenario of all the ingredients necessary to destroy these cities in a great fiery conflagration. Bitumen, asphalt, oil, gas—even salt to turn Lot's wife into a pillar. Another name for "brimstone," which Scripture says God "rained" upon these cities is sulfur, a major export of this region today. One need only consider the swiftness with which the ancient city of Pompeii met its doom via volcano to know something similar could have happened to these cities in such a volatile location.

The Dead Sea, in fact, lies in the northernmost extremity of The Great Rift, earth's longest valley, stretching from Syria in the north to Mozambique in the South. According to geologists, this interesting formation resulted from ground movement along a major fault line at some time anciently. *Encyclopedia Americana*, p. 351, says, "Outpourings of lava formed volcanic plateaus at places along the sides, as well as volcanoes in and near the valley" ("Great Rift Valley." Danbury, Connecticut: Grolier, 1983).

The devastation of Sodom and Gomorrah created a legend for centuries. Like Shiloh, the fate of those cities became an object lesson to Israel.

How God Destroyed the Cities

"Jerusalem stumbled, and Judah is fallen . . . They declare their sin as Sodom; they do not hide it. Woe to their soul! For *they have brought evil upon themselves*" (Isaiah 3:8,9;).

"The punishment of the iniquity of the daughter of my people is greater than the punishment of the sin of Sodom, which was overthrown in a moment, with no hand to help her!" (Lamentations 4:6. See also Isaiah 1: 9,10; Matthew 10:12-15; 11:23,24: Romans 9:29.)

Most revealing, however, is a familiar reference often quoted to depict the pain God feels at the death of sinners.

> How can I *give you up* Ephraim?
> How can I *hand you over*, Israel?
> How can I make you like Admah?
> How can I set you like Zeboiim?
> My heart churns within Me.
> My sympathy is stirred.
>
> (Hosea 11:8)

God uses the name Ephraim as a generic term in the same way He sometimes uses the name Judah, to denote an entire population.

No writer could more poignantly portray God's distress at the thought of "handing over" or "giving up" the nation to destruction, as He would one day *deliver up* the Sin-bearer to redeem a lost race. He compares such a prospect to the time He *gave up* and *handed over* Admah and Zeboiim.

Deuteronomy 29:23 and Genesis 14:2,8 give the names of all four cities destroyed when God poured fire upon the Cities of the Plain: Sodom, Gomorrah, Admah, and Zeboiim. According to Hosea, then, these last two cities, and by implication, Sodom and Gomorrah with them, were *handed over* and *given up* to destruction.

The depravity of these cities has become legendary, even down to our time. One city, Sodom, has lent its name to a practice clearly abhorrent to God, as evidenced by a number of Scriptural passages, among them Romans

1. The context shows that the apostle Paul understood "the wrath of God" to mean His reluctant departure from those whose ways show loyalty to the kingdom of darkness. Paul in Romans 1 speaks of those whom God *gave up* "to vile passions. For even their women exchanged the natural use for what is against nature. Likewise also the men, leaving the natural use of the woman, burned in their lust for one another, men with men committing what is shameful, and receiving in themselves the penalty of their error which was due. . . ." and "God *gave them over*" to the natural and inevitable consequences of their behavior. Paul's remarks in Romans 1 address a practice dating "from the creation of the world," clearly including the era of the Cities of the Plain.[19]

Nor does this exhaust the Biblical evidence that God *released* these cities to destruction rather than personally executing that destruction. Deuteronomy 29:23-28 strongly supports the "Release" position.

> The coming generation of your children who rise up after you and the foreigner who comes from a far land would say, when they see the plagues of that land and the sickness which the Lord has laid on it: "The whole land is brimstone, salt, and burning; it is not sown, nor does it bear, nor does any grass grow there, like the overthrow of Sodom and Gomorrah, Admah, and Zeboiim, which the Lord overthrew in His anger and His wrath."
>
> Then men would say: "Because they have forsaken the covenant of the Lord God of their fathers, which He made with them when He brought them out of the land of Egypt; for they went and served other gods and worshiped them, gods that they did not know and that He had not given to them.
>
> "Then *the anger of the Lord* was aroused against this land, to bring on it every curse that is written in this book. And the Lord uprooted them from their land in anger, in wrath, and in great indignation, and cast them into another land, as it is this day."

Here the prophet draws upon the past to predict the future. At the time God communicated this to Israel through Moses, Sodom and Gomorrah were an ancient legend, at least 400 years old. God wanted Israel to understand what would be the fate of the nation should she, like those cities, choose

---

[19]I did not invent this view of God; rather, I serve only as a reporter to call attention to a picture that the world has long misunderstood. In a work such as this, where God's love is magnified as never before, calling attention to the unsanctified nature of homosexuality cannot be interpreted to suggest that homosexuals should be harmed in any way. On the contrary, the picture is painted in kindness. And we have the positive assurance that the God who asks of us purity from the sins of the flesh, including homosexuality, offers with that request enabling power to overcome

to separate from God through sin. It is a fact of history that the nation did apostatize. After many centuries characterized by a cycle of apostasy, subjugation to surrounding nations, repentance, restoration, she eventually succumbed to the army of King Nebuchadnezzar of Babylon, who in 586 B. C. razed both the city of Jerusalem and the magnificent temple of Solomon within the city, killed or captured the people and transported many to Babylon.

But our text says there would be something similar in the way God destroyed the Israelite nation and the way in which He destroyed Sodom and Gomorrah. It says people will be struck by that similarity, implying more than mere visual likeness. The connotation is: Israel, be loyal to the covenant of God or you will suffer the same fate as Sodom and Gomorrah. Did He mean He would rain fire down from heaven upon them?

Israel was not loyal to God. She experienced all the adversity from which God tried to warn her. Since her fate corresponded with that of the Cities of the Plain, if we can discover God's role in the punishment of Israel, we shall also know the way in which He "rained brimstone and fire on Sodom and Gomorrah."

The Bible makes this revealing statement regarding the ignoble fate of this privileged and mighty nation at the hand of the king of Babylon:

> Zedekiah [the king] . . . did what is displeasing to Yahweh his God. He did not listen humbly to the prophet Jeremiah, accredited by Yahweh himself. He also rebelled against King Nebuchadnessar to whom he had sworn allegiance by God. He became stubborn and obstinately refused to return to Yahweh the God of Israel. Furthermore, all the heads of the priesthood, and the people too, added infidelity to infidelity, copying all the shameful practices of the nations and defiling the Temple that Yahweh had consecrated for himself in Jerusalem. Yahweh, the God of their ancestors, tirelessly sent them messenger after messenger, since he wished to spare his people and his house. But they ridiculed the messengers of God, they despised his words, they laughed at his prophets, until at last *the wrath of Yahweh* rose so high against his people that there was no further remedy.
>
> He summoned against them the king of the Chaldeans who put their young warriors to the sword within their sanctuary; he spared neither youth nor virgin, neither old man nor aged cripple; God *handed them all over* to him" (2 Chronicles 36:11-17, JB).

> "How can I *give you up*, Ephraim?
>   How can I *hand you over*, Israel?
>   How can I make you like Admah?
>   How can I set you like Zeboiim?

Here, again, God depicts Himself as *doing* what He does not prevent. He "summoned" the disaster, "spared neither" youth or aged. One might think God Himself personally inflicted this disaster upon His people. But no. The prophet Isaiah says in crystal-clear language that God "removed the protection of Judah" (Isaiah 22:8). As in the case of His own Son, the Sin-bearer, He simply ceased to protect, and the result? Release into the hands of destruction. Thus it was with Israel. And thus with Sodom.[20]

---

[20]This chapter appears very much as it was written more than a decade ago, during which time excavation in the region has continued. Contemporary accounts of archeological findings tend to support the conclusions within this chapter. To read current reports of what excavators have found and their conclusions regarding these findings, consult a library or the Internet, at sites such as:

http://www.abu.nb.ca/ecm/topics/arch5.htm

http://news.bbc.co.uk/hi/english/world/middle_east/newsid_1497000/1497476.stm

8

THOSE "HOLY" HEBREW WARS

"Then said Jesus unto him,
Put up again thy sword into his place:
for all they that take the sword
shall perish with the sword" (Matt. 26:52, KJV).

"Put up again thy sword," Jesus said to Peter. "All they that take the sword shall perish with the sword" (Matthew 26:52, KJV). At His mother's knee Jesus learned the eternal truths He later taught during the years of His adult ministry. His childhood textbook? The scrolls of the Hebrew Old Testament. How did His intimate connection with those often-violent writings shape His own nonviolent character? He must have seen in those stories something beyond the surface, so much so that in adulthood He could counsel Peter, Don't take in your hands the weapons of war and violence.[21]

Many through the centuries have wondered at the apparent contradiction between the character of Jesus and that of His Father. How could the gentle Jesus claim full oneness with that fierce Old Testament Being (John 10:30; 14:7-11) while lacking His warlike qualities?

Jesus "came unto His own, and His own received Him not" (John 1: 11, KJV). He was not what Israel expected or wanted in a Savior, when He came so different in character from the military Messiah they longed to herald. The puzzling contrast between Christ's character and that of the Old Testament God of war is so ancient that Christian thought today generally

---

[21]Today Christians tend to prefer the New Testament and make the Scriptures Jesus used subordinate to them. Why? Some claim Christian doctrine began with the New, an argument that weakens under scrutiny. See for example Deuteronomy 10:12; Jeremiah 31:33; Ezekiel 11:19; 18:31; 36:26, 27; John 3:10 (regarding new birth)

seems to have made peace with it. Since no one has known how to deal with it, the household of faith seems to agree to ignore it. But many cannot ignore it, and the preponderance of them are unbelievers. Must these be forever lost to the gospel? The good news is that this apparent dissonance *can* be understood and reconciled. Christianity can at last address this long overdue, unfinished item on its theological agenda.

According to Scripture, Jesus' character perfectly expressed that of the Godhead. When Jesus told Philip, "He who has seen Me has seen the Father," He identified Himself as the "base line" or standard. All else in Scripture (except the ten commandments) has passed through human hands and is therefore subject to misunderstanding. But not the character of Christ! The gospel writers describe His character clearly. Jesus came to reveal the Father, specifically *because we did not understand Him;* therefore, from the Christian point of view, we must reconcile the God of vengeance and wrath *to Him,* not the reverse.

We should expect to find, through close textual analysis, evidence of an alternate to the traditional view of the Old Testament God of war, bringing the apparent dissonance into harmony. Let us begin our study by returning to battlefields of old, seeking answers to this age-old riddle.

Slaves in Egypt

In the ancient land of Egypt a race of slaves, the Hebrews, served her kings and her commerce. Tradition among the slaves held that soon would come release. According to a promise made to their fathers by the God of heaven long ago, they would serve just 400 years in this foreign land and then depart with many possessions, and the 400 years drew steadily to a close.

How could the Egyptians ignore the rumor, which so energized the Hebrews with hope? Pharaoh determined to quench it permanently by invoking the "ultimate solution." The escape of Moses from this trap must have seemed providential, particularly when the daughter of Pharaoh spared his life, and his own mother took over his early training. He may have been about twelve when he moved into the palace and commenced his education as a soldier.

The Hebrews, separate yet a part of the Egyptian world, beheld all around them a mighty nation, made such through the strength of her military resources. Chariots, swords, horses, glittering garments of mail symbolized to these agrarian people the essential trappings of power. And here was their hero, Moses, in whom the nation's hopes lay, receiving as Pharaoh's grandson the highest military education available in the land. The timing was perfect.

And one day, to all appearances, the time arrived. Moses, out for a visit among his people, spied an Egyptian mistreating a Hebrew. Recklessly, without asking how it would affect his relations with the Egyptian throne, he slew the ruffian.

If he expected the Hebrews to thank him and rise up in revolution behind him, he overestimated their enthusiasm for freedom. Next day he learned just how isolated he was from the affections of Egyptians and Hebrews alike and, exercising great prudence, fled as far from both as his sandals would carry him.

Nonmilitary Exodus

Had God wanted a military solution to the problem of Hebrew bondage, here was His chance. But their emancipation was not to come in that way. Moses spent the next 40 years herding sheep on the rolling slopes of Midian, getting to know his Lord in a way not possible amid the sophistication of an Egyptian palace. When he had learned to walk and talk with God, when he had learned his own weakness, when he had learned to live in God, then God knew he was ready to lead.

And finally when he led the Israelites out of Egypt, they never drew a sword. God merely set up a situation where proud Pharaoh had to make a choice, to yield to His sovereignty or harden his heart in rebellion. When Pharaoh led the nation in declaring he "knew not God" and refused to comply with His instructions through Moses, his free-will decision and that of his subjects evicted God's protecting, sustaining presence from the nation, placing them in the power of the destroyer. But His canopy was over His people. The battle was His and all the glory was His own.

And evidence exists that He planned to take them into the Promised Land exactly as He brought them out of Egypt. "God did not lead them by way of the land of the Philistines, although that was near; for God said, 'Lest perhaps the people change their minds *when they see war* and return to Egypt'"; "The Lord your God, who goes before you, He will fight for you, according to all he did for you in Egypt before your eyes" (Exodus 13:17; Deuteronomy 1:30).

We have no record that the Israelites left Egypt equipped for war.[22] We do know that observation of the Egyptians conditioned them to equate power with military strength. We also know that somewhere along the exodus trail they acquired weapons, although the record does not say where. One commentator suggests they may have taken them off the Egyptians' dead

---

[22]The Hebrew in Exodus 13:18 states "by fifties" and therefore does not support the RSV translation "equpped for battle." Rather, the New King James rendering "in orderly ranks" expresses the original thought.

bodies, which washed up on the shore of the Red Sea the day after Pharaoh's ill-fated excursion through it (See Exodus 14:30).

Notice that God released the Hebrews from bondage in a very different way from that in which they subsequently entered Canaan. Could their wars of conquest have been an early example of the persistent rebellion that marked Israel's later years?

On one hand, God assumed full responsibility for defending the Hebrews, requiring of them only various nonmilitary acts of faith; for example, anointing doorposts with lamb's blood, walking down into the flowing Jordan, marching around Jericho—activities fully in keeping with the nonviolent character of Jesus. On the other hand, He commanded bloody military intervention. Were both His ideal will?

God's changelessness, Christ's benevolent character, and the track record of the people themselves suggest the latter may have been, not His ideal, but His best effort to cope with their persistent waywardness.[23]

Human Rebellion Against God

Where did Israel first obtain weapons? God had not so equipped them, according to the record. If they chose to be a military nation in spite of God's wish to protect them in His own way, would He not then have rejected them? Do we have a Biblical example showing what God might do under such circumstances?

It takes little thought to find such an example in the later history of the nation. Although God never intended Israel to have a visible king, He did not reject them when they claimed one. And their motive for this betrayal? "That we may be like all the nations" (1 Samuel 8:19). God warned them of the results of their choice, but He did not reject them for it. Did they, early on, desire to wage war "like" the Egyptians?

But in the case of their choosing a king, God expressed His disapproval. Do we have a Biblical example where humans defied God's ideal will *without* His expressing disapproval and also without His rejecting them for it? Yes.

In their practice of slavery and polygamy, which most Christians now agree were not in God's original plan.

---

[23]God apparently overlooked their ignorance here as He did in the case of polygamy, something He can no longer do in view of our close proximity to world's end. Scripture clearly depicts a people standing at that time "without fault" before the throne of God (Rev. 14:5), made so in part by an immense outpouring of crystal-clear truth in the final days, allowing them to order their lives according to it. Historically, our world has received a progression of heavenly light, which prophecy sees exploding upon the earth in fullness at the last.

Polygamy was so common among God's people in the Old Testament, examples need not be cited. Again, they thought to be "like" the surrounding nations, even though they knew God's perfect will for monogamous marriage had been beautifully expressed in the beginning (Genesis 2:20-24). But they chose to focus on their visible neighbors rather than on the invisible God, and beholding changed them into the same image (2 Corinthians 3:18). But nowhere do we find God railing against polygamy, although Christians today, with few exceptions, see the wrong of it.

The same could be said for slavery. The case against slavery rests upon God's commitment to the freedom and free will of His creatures. Both slavery and polygamy were God's permitted will for an antique age, never His ideal.

Could the Israelites themselves have chosen a military defense against God's ideal will, without His rejecting them for it, and also without Bible comment? The standard of Christ's character and three Biblical examples answer, Yes.

Language of Violence

But what about the terrible "killing" language God used in directing Israel to destroy the Canaanites? "You shall conquer them and utterly destroy them"; "You shall strike every male . . . with the edge of the sword. . . . Of the cities of these peoples which the Lord your God gives you as an inheritance, you shall let nothing that breathes remain alive, but you shall utterly destroy them" (Deuteronomy 7:2; 20:16, 17). If God's ideal will was something other than absolute destruction of the Canaanites by the sword of Israel, the language does not suggest it.

God invariably gives as a reason for the total annihilation of a people, "lest they teach you to do according to all their abominations which they have done for their gods and you sin against the Lord your God" (Deuteronomy 20:18).

Placing this language within our new model, God may be saying here and in numerous other places, in essence: You have chosen to deal with this emergency militarily, in harmony with the methods of the nations around you, instead of exercising the faith required to rely totally upon Me. Therefore, since you have chosen this method and I must either reject you for it or direct you in it, I choose to do the latter. When you go to these nations to war, you must utterly destroy them; otherwise, they will be a snare to you for all future generations. If you're going to do it your way, He seems to say, then do it right.[24]

Here, as in their later decision to have a king, the choice is final. They came to regret their request for a king (1 Kings 12:4,14), yet God neither reviewed nor revoked their servitude to one. Nor does He alter their choice to be a military nation.

It is interesting to note, through the perspective of time, that even here, following what may have been their own wayward choice, Israel proved unfaithful and ultimately reaped the predicted results of noncompliance with God's clear instructions. They failed to "utterly destroy" the Canaanites, who led them into idolatry and consequent separation from God from which the nation never fully recovered.

How might God have effected the Israelites' settlement in Canaan had they refused the sword? In our humanness we cannot see where they had a choice. Without it, what chance did they have against the armies of Canaan? But God always has other options.

God repeatedly informed the people He had no need of their swords (See, for example, Joshua 24:11,12; Psalm 44:3; Ezekiel 33:26), and the very first recorded combat between Israel and another nation underscores His point.

War With Amalek

The Amalekites came out to meet Israel at Rephidim in apparent cordiality. Then when the great mass of pilgrims had passed by, these villains fell in ambush upon the stragglers—the weak, the faint and the sick. Israel immediately mobilized for combat. Then, in one of the most noteworthy battles of the era, Moses, Aaron and Hur ascended a nearby hill. As the battle raged, Moses stood upon the hilltop, his staff raised toward heaven. While he maintained this posture, Israel prevailed. But if he lowered the staff, Amalek triumphed. As the battle wore on, Moses could not maintain his winning stance alone. Therefore, Aaron and Hur found a large stone, sat him on it and held up his arms until Amalek was vanquished (Exodus 17:8-16; Deuteronomy 25:17-19).

Israel's instant mobilization here suggests that the issue of how they were to defend themselves in event of enemy attack had already been discussed and settled. They had weapons, though the Bible doesn't say where they got them. If God wanted to make a statement emphasizing their dependence upon

---

[24]Scripture contains further evidence that in many cases God could not deal with Israel according to His perfect will. See for example Ezekiel 20:25 and Matthew 19:8

His power rather than upon their military prowess, a position He maintains throughout the Old Testament, He couldn't have said it better than He said it here.

If they had eschewed weapons and relied fully upon the care of God, how would they have handled Amalek's aggression? Would God have approved their lack of response to this crisis?

Who can say whether this crisis would have arisen, had the nation internalized that God is faithful and let Him take care of it. Whether they made a deliberate choice to take the sword, or whether their persistent rebellion simply removed them from His authority, disobedience obligated the nation to a different set of circumstances and experiences than she would have known under God's sole management. The decision to take the sword may have been simply another step in a series of rebellious choices, which progressively removed them from God's jurisdiction. Neither this incident nor any other combat situation in which Israel engaged was more threatening to them than the circumstances of their exit from Egypt, an event demanding a military solution—if there ever was one—from a human point of view.

God kept the events of their release from bondage continually before them to emphasize His power to defend them with weapons to which they had no access. "If you should say in your heart, 'These nations are greater than I; how can I dispossess them?' You shall not be afraid of them, but remember well what the Lord your God did to Pharaoh and to all Egypt: the great signs and the wonders, the mighty hand and the outstretched arm. . . . Moreover the Lord your God will send the hornet among them until those who are left, who hide themselves from you, are destroyed" (Deuteronomy 7: 17-20).

But hornets, or the natural phenomena the hornets may also symbolize, were only one of God's many options. Scripture abounds with illustrations of the shelter God provides.

Living By Faith

When Moab, Ammon, and Mount Seir came to war against good king Jehoshaphat, he might have trusted in the extensive fortifications built during his reign, but this he did not do. His method of dealing with this crisis contains all the Biblical elements of living by faith. He gathered the nation in a great prayer meeting. Lifting his voice to the God of might, he praised Him for past blessings, recognized His position at the head of the nation, claimed His promises in the past and briefly described the present emergency. God communicated with a prophet on the spot, promising Jehoshaphat and his people that the battle was not theirs but His. On the basis of this promise, while it was still just a promise, the people claimed victory and went singing to battle, armed alone with the mighty weapon of praise. "Now when the people began to sing and to praise, the Lord set ambushes against the people of Ammon, Moab, and Mount Seir, who had come against Judah; and they were defeated. For the people of Ammon and Moab stood up against the inhabitants of Mount Seir to utterly kill and destroy them. And when they had made an end of the inhabitants of Seir, they helped to destroy one another" (2 Chronicles 20:22, 23. See also 1 Samuel 14; 2 Kings 7).

This is just one of many stories that could be cited, showing God's power to deliver His faithful people without their resorting to force of arms. We need fear no limitation in God's repertoire of strategies for defending His people, if we place the full weight of our faith upon His everlasting might.

Their Protection Has Departed

Correctly understood, the Canaanite dispossession had nothing whatever to do with Hebrew military prowess.[25] God had delayed the settlement of Abraham's descendants in the Promised Land until "the fourth generation," because "the iniquity of the Amorites [Canaanites]" was "not yet complete" in Abraham's day (Genesis 15:16). God would not encroach on Canaanite land on behalf of Israel while any hope existed that the indigenous people would yield to righteousness. The same rule existed for them as for all nations, for God "has made from one blood every nation of men to dwell on all the face of the earth and has determined their preappointed times and the boundaries of their habitation so that they should seek the Lord, in the hope

---

[25]Numerous Scriptural reasons exist to believe God never intended Israel to defend themselves militarily. To recap this key point:

1) Jesus never addressed His enemies with weapons of war. In fact, He forbade it. Weight this point more heavily than all others combined. (See Matt. 5:43-45; 26:52; Rev. 13:10).

2) God did not intend Israel to engage in war on her journey to the Promised Land (Exodus 13:17; Deut. 1:30-32).

3) God was in no way indebted to Israel's sword for their possession of the Promised Land (Psalm 44:3; Jeremiah 33:26; Deut. 3:22).

4) God gave them flawed instructions due to their hardness of heart (Ezekiel 20:25; Matt. 5: 21-48; 19:8).

5) Victory always turned on their obedience to God, not their military might (Zech. 4:6; 1 Kings 9:3-9).

6) God intended to protect His people through the arsenal of nature, as He did in releasing them from Egyptian bondage (Exodus 23:27-30).

7)When Israel compromised by contracting multiple marriages, holding slaves and demanding a king, He did not reject them for it. He tried to install principles and requirements to make the best of a less-than-perfect situation, likely following the same procedure in regard to their choice to take up arms (Exodus 21:2-11; 1 Samuel 8).

that they might grope for Him and find Him, though He is not far from each one of us; for in Him we live and move and have our being" (Acts 17:26-28).

Faithful Caleb showed he understood this principle, when Israel rebelled on the very borders of the Promised Land. He said, "Do not rebel against the Lord nor fear the people of the land. . . . *their protection has departed from them*, and the Lord is with us" (Numbers 14:9). Caleb recognized in the exodus the signal that these nations had sinned away their day of grace, that God could no longer reach them with salvation, that their final moral choice had removed them from God's authority and consequent protection.

Moses elaborates on this fact in Deuteronomy 9:1,4,5: "Hear, O Israel: You are to cross over the Jordan today, and go in to dispossess nations greater and mightier than yourself, cities great and fortified up to heaven. . . Do not think in your heart, after the Lord your God has cast them out before you, saying 'Because of my righteousness the Lord has brought me in to possess this land'. . . . It is not because of your righteousness or the uprightness of your heart that you go in to possess their land, but because of the wickedness of these nations that the Lord your God drives them out from before you."

Through their commitment to rebellion against the principles of God's kingdom, the Canaanites rejected their only source of protection and life. Thus the record repeatedly declares that God "handed them over," "delivered them up," or "abandoned" them to the sword of Israel. But God declares, and their experience shows, He was in no way beholden to Hebrew military power. The same principles functioned in the Canaanite dispossession as have always existed where God's creatures have free will. Our patient God bears long, so very long, with human self-sufficiency and independence from Himself. In mercy He remains to provide for and protect humans who haven't the slightest sense of their indebtedness to Him. But the time comes when their decision is final, their commitment to independence of Him unchangeable. Choosing to separate from Him, they become vulnerable to death, for *there is no life apart from God.*

9

WHAT REALLY CAUSED NOAH'S FLOOD?

"My Spirit shall not always strive with man" (Gen. 6:3).

"And God said to Noah, 'The end of all flesh has come before Me, for the earth is filled with violence through them; and behold, I will destroy them with the earth. . . .

"I Myself am bringing the flood of waters on the earth, to destroy from under heaven all flesh in which is the breath of life; and everything that is on the earth shall die'" (Genesis 6:13, 17).

Thus begins a story familiar to anyone possessing the slightest acquaintance with the Judeo-Christian tradition. Few legends of antiquity provoke more controversy than the story of Noah and the flood.

While we do not know enough to be dogmatic about how Noah's flood took place, we have enough information to make a good case that it followed the same principles involved in other Biblical examples of God's wrath.

Nothing in scientific fact refutes this Bible story (although "scientific" philosophy may smile it to scorn). Individuals desiring further study will wish to obtain the book, *The Genesis Flood*, by John C. Whitcombe, Jr., and Henry M. Morris (Philadelphia: Presbyterian and Reformed Publishing Company), a standard work and comprehensive defense of the Biblical story of the flood based on current scientific knowledge. The following account relates to the way in which such a flood could have occurred. Did God personally execute the antediluvians by drowning, or did they "run Him off," depriving themselves of His protection?

Creation

In order to understand what took place at the flood, we must first look at some of the details of creation.

On the second day, "God said, 'Let there be a firmament in the midst of the waters, and let it divide the waters from the waters.' Thus God made the firmament [where the birds fly, v. 20], and divided the waters which were under the firmament from the waters which were above the firmament; and it was so" (Genesis 1:6,7).

Modern readers of these words can become confused as to their meaning, for while they seem to describe recognizable conditions on our earth, they fail to correlate with anything we see above us today.

Yet Genesis insists that during creation week God "sandwiched" the sky (as we know it) between two great bodies of water—one on, in, and under the earth, and the other above that great heavenly expanse. Something upheld that canopy of water above the sky, screening the sun's harmful rays and diffusing light and warmth evenly upon the earth's surface, producing a "greenhouse effect," very unlike the one we read of in newspapers today. Evidently the dual powers of the pre-deluge sun and moon exerted drawing power on this canopy, much as the sun draws tons of water into the skies today by evaporation, forming clouds.

"A mist went up from the earth and watered the whole face of the ground" (Genesis 2:6). Water simply recycled in the area between these two great layers of water, much as it would in a terrarium.

The apostle Peter describes the old world as earth and sky, each in water and out of water (2 Peter 3:5), an enigmatic statement indeed to try to match with today's conditions, yet matching perfectly with the description of earth as it emerged from the Creator's hand.

The obvious question at this point is: What happened to all that water above the earth?

The Sun and Moon

The Bible speaks of a time yet future when God will re-create our battered world. "The light of the moon will be as the light of the sun, and the light of the sun will be sevenfold, as the light of seven days, in the day that the Lord binds up the bruise of His people and heals the stroke of their wound" (Isaiah 30:26).

In restoring the original creation, it appears that God will restore the moon's radiance until it is as the light of the sun. We may conclude from this that our moon was once a self-luminous body as bright as our present sun. Moon rocks gathered during space missions do not rule out their possible igneous origin.

Further, the light of the restored sun, much farther from the earth than the moon, will shine seven times brighter than now, suggesting that the pre-flood sun was seven times brighter than today.

It has been suggested that both moon and sun emitted exactly the right amount of heat in relation to their distance from the earth, the "vapor mantle," and each other to balance this great blanket of water above the antediluvian sky, in a constant stationary "orbit." This canopy, in turn, protected earth-life from the immense temperatures created by these giant generators, absorbing the heat evenly, and distributing just the right amount to maintain a perfect climate over the entire surface of the globe.

Meantime down below, humans fortunate enough to live in this lush paradise were taking it all for granted. Rather than thanking God, they turned from Him in an orgy of self-indulgence.

The Genesis Flood says this regarding the times: "The constant, almost monotonous repetition of [Biblical] phrases depicting the utter depravity of antediluvian humanity has filled the minds of believers with a sense of awe and astonishment. Every statement seems calculated to impress upon its readers the idea of universal sin, not just the exceptional sins of this group or of that region, nor even of specific times or occasions, but rather the sins of an entire age and an entire race that had utterly corrupted its way upon the earth and was now ripe for the judgment of a holy God" (p. 18). And judgment came, but how?

Grieving the Holy Spirit

In a statement that, until now, seemed strangely out of place in the Scriptural account of the flood, God says regarding this world of universal evil, "My Spirit shall not strive with man forever" (Genesis 6:3). The apostle Peter adds that the Holy Spirit "preached" to disobedient "spirits in prison" (lost humans) while God waited patiently for Noah to complete the ark (1 Peter 3:18-20). These and other references clarify the vital role of the Holy Spirit in antediluvian times.

Scripture depicts God as controlling and sustaining nature, not as an "absentee Landlord" but as a present Power working in and through natural law to sustain, protect, and perpetuate life. Here in the world before the flood, the adversary had won virtually a complete victory. But the Spirit remained, supporting nature and speaking in His characteristic "still small voice" to the peoples' inner consciousness, "waiting patiently." As Noah's steady hammer blows drove nails into the ark, the Spirit drove a question into human minds. "I wonder if he's right?"

But the undercurrent of conviction gave way to conformity, for surface public opinion held Noah in contempt. When the ark was completed only eight people believed God and entered. According to the "rules of the contest" and in harmony with His commitment to the free will of His creatures, God had no fair choice but to back off. The command went forth, "Release."

What happened next may not be known in its fullness this side of eternity. This work is not a scientific treatment of the subject. Rather, we are exploring whether the same principles operated at Noah's flood as at other events historically understood as "acts of God." We cannot conclude here;

we can only theorize. Following are some ideas as to the way in which this disaster may have occurred.

Absent its energy Source, the moon ceased generating its own light, went out, and became a reflector of the sun. For the same reason the sun diminished to its present intensity, upset the balance supporting the water mantle, and contrary to the best "scientific" projections, rain poured down. Asteroid or meteorite activity may have played a part as well. The Bible also records a "breaking up" of the "great deep" at that time, suggesting great and powerful jets bursting forth from the waters on and under the earth's crust. Whether God's withdrawal precipitated each of these effects, or whether, domino-like, release of the water canopy, asteroids or meteorites initiated further disasters, which God declined to prevent, we do not know. We do know that, due to the devastation and to atmospheric and other changes dating from that period, life on earth has not been the same since.

We also know that, following the flood, the saving of righteous Noah and his family tipped the scales back to God's side, giving Him authority to continue His rescue work for the human race. The earth was again, to a great degree, At-One with its Creator.

Scripture promises a future when that rescue work will end in victory and humans will enjoy a restored creation. The sun and moon figure heavily in those promises. Those bodies will return to their original intensity, and "Your sun shall no longer go down [diminish in power], nor shall your moon withdraw itself" (Isaiah 60:20). Yet "the Lord will be to you an everlasting light, and your God your glory" (Isaiah 60:19). No orb in the sky will engross the attention of the redeemed above the glory of their mighty Redeemer!

> "For a mere moment I have *forsaken* you,
>> But with great mercy I will gather you.
>>> With a little *wrath I hid My face*
>>>> from you for a moment;
>> But with everlasting kindness
>>> I will have mercy on you,"
>>>> Says the Lord, your Redeemer.
> "For this is *like the waters of Noah to M*e;
> For as I have sworn that the waters of Noah would no longer cover the earth,
>> So have I sworn that
>>> I would not be *angry* with you."
>>>> (Isaiah 54:7-9)[26]

---

[26]In an interesting sidelight from the book of Job, written within a few generations of the flood, Eliphaz asks: *(Continued on page 73)*

<table>
<tr>
<td>
10
</td>
<td>

THE CASE OF KORAH

"Love your enemies, bless those who curse you, do good to those who hate you, and pray for those who spitefully use you and persecute you, that you may be sons of your Father in heaven" (Matt. 5:44).

</td>
</tr>
</table>

No Israelites died leaving Egypt. In all the solemn, threatening events leading to their release, we have no record that any of them perished. But the same cannot be said for their journey toward the Promised Land. It is an interesting exercise to find and list the occasions on which, contrary to God's apparent plan, the people perished.

What made the difference? It seemed to come down to the fact that in learning to speak, they had never learned the language of heaven, which has no words for complaining against God.

(Continuation)   Will you keep to the old way
             Which wicked men have trod,
      Who were cut down before their time,
          Whose foundations were swept away by a flood?
        They said to God, "Depart from us!"
         What can the Almighty do?(Job 22:15-17)

This statement, along with several others from Job's "friends," suggest they, like the modern world in general, recognized the principle of human separation from God, but they, as we, failed to understand that when this alienation becomes incurable, God does, in fact, depart. He does not then return to execute revenge against His enemies. Job alone expressed an embryonic knowledge of this dynamic (See Chapter 5). The book of Job may afford fertile ground for future investigation relating to the present topic.

Could they complain! First they were thirsty, then hungry. Their expectations never allowed for an omnipotent, loving God on their side. Their lives were so dear to them, that in seeking their preservation, as at Kadesh-Barnea, they died anyway. Few seemed willing to stake their lives on God's faithfulness.

Into this picture enter Korah, a Levite and prince of Israel, plus Dathan, Abiram and On,[26] all leaders among the people, plus two hundred fifty princes of Israel, who took it upon themselves to "murmur" against Aaron and to challenge the leadership of Moses.

"You take too much upon yourselves [Moses and Aaron], for all the congregation is holy, every one of them, and the Lord is among them. Why then do you exalt yourselves above the congregation of the Lord?" (Numbers 16:3).

Challenged to a showdown, Moses suggests that the principals stand before the tabernacle with censers in their hands, and let God decide the issue. God then instructs Moses, "Tell everyone to stand away from the tents of Korah, Dathan, and Abiram."

Moses so instructs the people.

"Then Moses said: 'By this you shall know that the Lord has sent me to do all these works, for I have not done them of my own will. If these men die naturally like all men, or if they are visited by the common fate of all men, then the Lord has not sent me. But if the Lord creates a new thing and the earth opens its mouth and swallows them up with all that belongs to them and they go down alive into the pit, then you will understand that these men have rejected the Lord.'

"Then it came to pass, as he finished speaking all these words, that the ground split apart under them. And the earth opened its mouth and swallowed them up, with their households and all the men with Korah, with all their goods. So they and all those with them went down alive into the pit; the earth closed over them, and they perished from among the congregation. . . . And a fire came out from the Lord and consumed the two hundred and fifty men who were offering incense" (Numbers 16:28-35).

Traditionally, we have taken this episode at face value. They rebelled. God, to maintain order and confirm the leadership of Moses and Aaron, split open the earth and destroyed the rebels. Then He finished off the two hundred fifty with fire.

By now we know that in the invisible world, events may have occurred not described here. If God released an earthquake all primed to happen

---

[27]Lack of further reference to On hints he may have repented.

beneath their feet at that exact moment, He could certainly have communicated that fact to Moses. Fire often accompanies earthquakes, as at Pompei, San Francisco, etc. Nothing in the description precludes our alternate view. But do we have any other Scriptural support in this matter?

The Counsel of Paul

Regarding the exodus, the apostle Paul counsels, "Do not become idolaters as were some of them. . . . Nor let us commit sexual immorality, as some of them did, and in one day twenty-three thousand fell; nor let us tempt Christ, as some of them also tempted, and were destroyed by serpents; nor murmur, as some of them also murmured, and were destroyed by the [*definite article*] destroyer" (1 Corinthians 10:7-10).

It appears the apostle does not intend to leave anyone out. In indexing the deaths on that long journey toward the Promised Land, they all seem to fit in here somewhere. Note. . .

"Do not become idolaters as were some of them (See Exodus 32). . . . Nor let us commit sexual immorality, as some of them did, and in one day twenty-three thousand fell (See Numbers 25:1-9); nor let us tempt Christ, as some of them also tempted, and were destroyed by serpents (See Numbers 21:6-9); nor murmur, as some of them also murmured, and were destroyed by the destroyer."

And we know who he is.

The last entry of complainers, destroyed by the destroyer, includes the quail eaters (See Exodus 16, Numbers 11), the Kadesh-Barnea rebels (See Numbers 13, 14; Deuteronomy 1:19-46; 2:14-16); and Korah, Dathan and Abiram (See Numbers 16, 17).

The Unforgivable Sin

This interpretation of the story of Korah, Dathan and Abiram generates more criticism than probably any other aspect of this new view of God. Critics say the destruction of Korah and his supporters was clearly a work of God, and those who see more in the story are doing the devil's work in blaming the devil for this rebellion and its aftermath. They wonder how it can be said that Satan destroyed these rebels, when *God obviously executed* their death sentence. To call a work of God a work of Satan conforms to the definition of the unforgivable sin, they say.

However, their argument is not with this interpretation of the story; it is with the apostle Paul, who said that Korah, Dathan and Abiram were destroyed by "the" (*definite article*) destroyer.

Consider these facts:

- The position described in these pages is not proved solely with this incident; therefore, it cannot be disproved solely by attacking this one point. If the view is wrong, it must be disproved from A to Z.

- If that *cannot* be done, it may be that God is sending advanced light to our world. Then *who is committing the sin against the Holy Ghost by rejecting that light?*

- The incident could have happened either way—as traditionally believed or as described in *Light On the Dark Side of God*, if all we go by is evidence existing in the text. The context doesn't show God splitting open the earth.

Who put the envy into Korah's heart? Whence came his boldness to challenge the leadership of God's appointed servants? Is it not interesting that Scriptural evidence exists that allows this incident to be described in terms of the alternate view? These men had rejected the Lord. Satan, the first cause in any sinful program, whispered thoughts to rebel hearts that lead them on to separation from God and consequent disaster, thus they were "destroyed by the destroyer."

God merely lost authority to prevent their destruction. (Physically He could have prevented it, but the exercise of the rebels' free will tied His hands.) He told Moses what aspect of nature He had released, as He told Satan in the story of Job. In both cases, God got the blame (See Job 2:3, 5).

11

WHAT IS THE END-TIME WRATH OF GOD?

"He that leadeth into captivity shall go into captivity:
he that killeth with the sword must be killed with the sword.
Here is the patience and the faith of the saints" (Rev. 13:10).

The difference in religions lies in the character of the one each calls "God." The doctrines and rituals of the church, which on the surface seem to define it, on closer view flow out of its picture of Deity. Our religious differences exist because we do not serve the same god. A mean-spirited, arbitrary god makes illogical demands on believers and relates to them in bewildering ways, sometimes driving them mad trying to "measure up." A reasonable, compassionate God makes sense; He exacts nothing from the believer; He only reveals Himself, and the vision attracts the human heart to know and follow Him.

The idea of "the wrath of God," so prominent in Scripture has lent itself through the centuries to a fearful picture of the Bible's God, with perhaps the most damaging charges centering on His end-time wrath. We have already defined the Biblical concept of "the wrath of God," and there is no reason to think that definition changes in earth's last days. But since the warnings in Scripture against end-time wrath may have special meaning for us, it behooves us to take a closer look at it.

Daniel and Revelation Speak

In the book of Revelation, references to final wrath occur thirteen times. A typical example reads, "If anyone worships the beast and his image, and receives his mark on his forehead or on his hand, he himself shall also drink of the wine of the wrath of God which is poured out full strength into the cup of His indignation" (Revelation 14:9, 10). Whatever God's end-time wrath is, it doesn't bode well for the sinner.

The book of Daniel also mentions "the wrath" in the same end-time context as Revelation (for example, Daniel 8:19; 10:14; 11:36). It is an interesting exercise to read through the small book of Daniel and mark the statements mentioning "the end." Clearly, both the book of Daniel and the book of Revelation describe final wrath and address in particular those living in earth's last days.[28]

Although "wrath" occurred from time to time throughout history, this era is called "the end," in recognition of the consequences of a final episode of "wrath" upon our planet. "At that time…there shall be a time of trouble, *such as never was since there was a nation, even to that time*" (Daniel 12:1). "For then there shall be great tribulation, such as has not been since the beginning of the world until this time, no, nor ever shall be (Matthew 24:21).

Revelation adds, "Then I heard a loud voice from the temple saying to the seven angels, 'Go and pour out the bowls of the wrath of God on the earth'" (16:1), an event signaling the start of the seven last plagues. In these bowls "the wrath of God is complete" (15:1), perhaps indicating that Mercy can no longer legally block sin's natural consequences, for human free will has knowingly accepted sin on a worldwide scale. "*All* the world marveled and followed the beast." "*All* who dwell on the earth will worship him" (the beast, Revelation 13:3, 8;), giving loyalty to peer pressure and public opinion and despising the will of God clearly revealed in His word. Which way will we choose in that day? "The wrath of God" has a last-days application to which other episodes of "wrath" were but a prelude.

End-time Wrath

The Bible underscores the horror of final wrath with descriptions such as these: "Behold, the day of the Lord comes, cruel with both wrath and fierce anger, to lay the land desolate; and He will destroy its sinners from it. . . . Therefore I will shake the heavens, and the earth will move out of her place, in the wrath of the Lord of hosts and in the day of His fierce anger" (Isaiah 13:9,13).

On the surface, statements such as these appear to depict God as One who brings chaos, suffering and pain into earth's environment at a magnitude which unfits it to sustain human life. Even the supremely compassionate and merciful Jesus warned of this coming "wrath." "He who believes in the Son has everlasting life; and he who does not believe in the Son shall not see life, but the wrath of God abides on him" (John 3:36).

After sacrificing His Son to give us hope, will God, in the final act, horribly torture and execute those who decline His generosity? How can this be? Are we obliged to approve in God that which we would abhor in humans? Again, given our traditional understanding of His wrath, we see

---

[28]In that connection Jesus predicted "wars and rumors of wars" as "the beginning of sorrows," "but the end is not yet" (Matt. 24:6, 8). No, but "when they say 'peace and safety,' *then* sudden destruction comes upon them. . . . And they shall not escape" (1 Thess. 5:2).

a God who is both arbitrary and bloodthirsty, granting freedom of choice but intending to punish those who do not choose Him. He confuses us. The human response has ranged from universalism (the idea that these descriptions are all metaphors and all humans will at last be saved) to mind numbing acceptance of all that doesn't make sense, to full rejection manifesting in secularism and atheism.

Could it be that now, at world's end, God is sweeping away the fog in order that we might make our final choices based upon a clear and accurate picture of His character?

Although abundant Scriptural references exist which appear to designate God as the agent of wrath, at least as many references present it in a very different way. The following examples almost objectify "wrath" as an entity having an existence of its own:

- The Levites shall camp around the tabernacle of the Testimony, that there may be no wrath on the congregation of the children of Israel (Numbers 1:53).

- This we will do to them: we will let them live, lest wrath be upon us because of the oath which we swore to them (Joshua 9:20).

- Joab the son of Zeruiah began a census, but he did not finish, for wrath came upon Israel because of this census (1 Chronicles 27:24).

- Whatever is commanded by the God of heaven, let it diligently be done for the house of the God of heaven. For why should there be wrath against the realm of the king and his sons? (Ezra 7:23).

Is "wrath" a product of God's willful activity, or does it have an existence separate from Him, an existence where He is, in actual fact, absent?

Further, the emotion "wrath" or "anger" is not in the traditional sense an attribute of Deity. "The works of the flesh are evident, which are: adultery, fornication, uncleanness, licentiousness, idolatry, sorcery, hatred, contentions, jealousies, . . . *wrath*, selfish ambitions, dissensions, heresies, envy, murders, drunkenness, revelries, and the like. . . . Those who practice such things will not inherit the kingdom of God" (Galatians 5:19-21).

Finally, the Biblical picture of "wrath" would not be complete without noting a reference in the book of Revelation to the wrath of Satan (Rev.12:12). Biblical evidence invites theologians to re-study this topic. As Christians, we need to offer the world a better picture of the gospel than we have offered in the past, a picture that is both Scriptural and reasonable, a picture that sees sinners punished, while absolving God of any actions inconsistent with His character of love.

Biblical Keys

With that background we are now ready to look for Biblical keys to understanding God's role in final wrath. We have already explored some general principles. Can we find other helpful illustrations? Can we establish a connection between Biblical episodes of "wrath" and end-time "wrath?" Keep in mind the angel of Revelation who cries, "If anyone worships the beast and his image, and receives his mark on his forehead or on his hand, he himself shall also drink of the wine of the wrath of God, which is poured out full strength into the cup of His indignation."

Note the similarity with the following Old Testament quotation: "For thus says the Lord God of Israel to me: 'Take this wine cup of fury [wrath] from My hand, and cause all the nations to whom I send you to drink it. And they will drink and stagger and go mad because of the sword that I will send among them' Then I took the cup from the Lord's hand, and made all the nations drink, to whom the Lord had sent me" (Jeremiah 25:15).

Who were the "nations" to whom God sent the prophet Jeremiah? He mentions several, but none possess as complete a Biblical history as the first mentioned. Therefore, we shall examine the fate of Jerusalem, a city which appears to have suffered "wrath" at two different times in her history.

Jeremiah 25 concerns the first episode in 586 B. C., already mentioned in connection with the destruction of Sodom. Here as in so many other places the surface language suggests destruction through God's personal intervention. He will "bring evil" on the city (v. 29). He will bring Nebuchadnezzaar of Babylon against the land (v. 9).

However, the context also reveals another dynamic operating in the destruction of Jerusalem anciently. God *left* His shelter as a lion leaves his "covert" or "lair" (v. 38;). [Psalm 76:2 says, "In Salem (Jerusalem) also is His tabernacle, and His dwelling place in Zion" (another name for Jerusalem).] He will *"give* those who are wicked to the sword" (v. 31). God's departure from the city exposed it to its enemy, Babylon.

Some seventy years after Nebuchadnezzar captured Jerusalem, Ezra the priest records a fact generally known among the Hebrews returning from captivity to rebuild the city. "Because our fathers provoked the God of heaven to wrath, He *gave them into* the hand of Nebuchadnezzar, king of Babylon"(Ezra 5:12;). Other texts as well indicate that the city fell, not because God personally brought it down, but because He was not there to uphold it. God did not choose this fate for Jerusalem; rather, the people chose to separate from Him, and our gracious God deferred to their free will.

Christians believe the kingdom of God suffered a major rejection in Jerusalem just a few short years before 70 A.D. In the course of this rejection, note, the high priest, Caiaphas, tore his robes, which Jewish law from the beginning strictly forbade. "He who is the high priest among his brethren… shall not uncover his head nor tear his clothes." "And Moses said to Aaron [the high priest], and to Eleazar and Ithamar, his sons, 'Do not uncover your heads nor tear your clothes, lest you die, and wrath come upon all the people" (Mark 14:63; Leviticus 21:10; 10:6). Caiaphas may have thought to signify his dismay at Christ's claim to Deity; however, long-standing Jewish tradition viewed the tearing of the high priest's garments as a symbol of separation from God.

Before Jesus ever embarked on His own ministry, his cousin, John the Baptist, warned the people to repent and flee from the "wrath to come." To what did the Baptist refer?

It is true, in a sense, that all the lost must face final wrath. "The wicked… shall be brought forth [resurrected] to the day of wrath" (Job 21:30). The apostle Paul says, "Jesus delivered us [converts to His kingdom] from the wrath to come" (1 Thessalonians 1:10).

But could John the Baptist have meant to warn the city to cherish her final opportunity for repentance through Jesus? Might he have had in mind the impending destruction of Jerusalem in 70 A.D. when he warned of "the wrath to come?" Significantly, in prophesying regarding the future destruction of Jerusalem, Jesus said, "There will be great distress in the land, and wrath upon the people" (Luke 21:23). It seems clear that the same factors which destroyed Jerusalem in 586 B.C. destroyed her again in 70 A.D.[29]

Great Past Civilizations

And what of the great civilizations of the ancient past? Greece? Rome? A correlation has long been noted between the deteriorating morals of these great cultures and their final demise. Although we have no specific documentation supporting it, we cannot but wonder if the principles here set

---

[29]Some challenge this view on the basis that God and Satan never collaborate. When God releases humans, some find it puzzling to understand how God induces the enemy, at that exact moment, to do the destroying work. When considering this new picture of wrath, they seem to see God whistling up the adversary to call his attention to the fact that here are some exposed humans for his lethal entertainment. He wants them destroyed, and now! The enemy sashays over, surveys the situation; they negotiate a bit. Finally, at God's insistence, the enemy executes sentence upon the transgressor. This is not what is being suggested.

Imagine the wind blowing through a tree of very ripe apples. A stem snaps. What happens? Does gravity call to the apple to descend to earth? Do they spend time negotiating the details? No. Without a stem to hold it, the apple falls to earth. It cannot resist gravity in its own strength. It falls, because that's what apples with broken stems do. *(Footnote continued on page 82)*

out were involved in bringing them down. Could the era of history known as the French Revolution be described in similar terms?

Up to now it has seemed as if there were no accountability for what secularism, sin and man-made religion have done to the human race. Or, if accountability has seemed to exist at all, we thought God meted it out when He reached His "boiling point." But now it appears there is a fail-safe punishment built into the very fabric of transgression itself.

But who bears responsibility for that punishment—God or humans? We do not stay where the atmosphere is uncomfortable to us. God does, but only up to a point. When human free will pushes Him away forever, God leaves. He has no choice. *Legally* He has no choice. *Morally* He has no choice. It's the law. Humans choose their own master. Otherwise, our ever-courteous God takes on the aspect of a bully, either forcing Himself into the company of those who despise Him or altering His character to accommodate wickedness, and that our changeless God can never do.

But before departing He brings all the strength of His powers of persuasion to bear upon our hearts, to convince you and me to live. "I have no pleasure in the death of the wicked, but that the wicked turn from his way and live. Turn, turn from your evil ways! For why should you die?" (Ezekiel 33:11).

The very nature of human existence requires a Lifegiver, not simply to initiate life but to sustain it as well. When God loses authority to *maintain* that existence, when human free will obliges Him to depart for the final time, chaos reigns. When God tells the lost, "Depart from me, I never knew you," there is *nothing worse*. We cannot imagine in our wildest nightmares what will happen when the wicked realize they are lost—inexcusably and eternally lost. We cannot envision their terror when this planet burns. *Words cannot convey it.* Any punishment we might imagine for the devil himself will not reach the magnitude of the event, when "all nations drink of the wine of the wrath of God" (Revelation 14:10). But God Himself will be ever free of any taint of responsibility in the matter. Free will is such a precious thing in His sight.

(Continued from page 81)

Or imagine a sudden breach in a dam. What happens to the water? It flows through; natural law dictates the consequences of having a hole in a dam.

Similarly, the enemy destroys. God is our hedge against him. When that hedge is breached, for whatever reason, nothing prevents Satan from exercising his character, which is destructive. Will he always destroy when the hedge is breached? Yes, unless it is to his advantage to delay awhile. This permits him to use his own agents as bait to tempt others into sin. He particularly seems to relish destroying when he can blame God for it. But make no mistake about it; willful sin in the life exposes humans to the destroyer. And Satan will, sooner or later, exercise his destructive nature against his servant, the sinner.

12

HELLFIRE RECONSIDERED

"I brought fire from your midst.
It devoured you. And I turned you to ashes
upon the earth in the sight of all who saw you"
(Ezekiel 28:18).

Christianity is divided on many issues, but on one she enjoys great unanimity—that God will destroy the unsaved in a blazing holocaust.

Heaven sacrificed its richest Treasure to relieve humans of this fate, but one thing Heaven cannot do for humans—make their decision to live. Tragically many will not choose life and the ways of God's eternal kingdom; therefore, Scripture decrees fire as their final end. Is this God's arbitrary decision? Is He saying, Serve Me or I'll burn you? How is this different from the pagan King Nebuchadnezzar's ordering three young Hebrew men to worship his way, or he would have them thrown into a "burning, fiery furnace?" (Read the story in Daniel 3.)

Or is it possible that sin, in the final act, comes full circle and destroys itself, this time by fire, while God's real position is that He pleads Calvary's blood to woo sinners away from such a fate?

The churches of Christendom generally agree that a lake of fire burns somewhere in eternity, awaiting the souls and spirits of the lost. While some Biblical statements appear on the surface to support such a view, the position fails to consider the *full range* of Scriptural statements on this point, including many which depict "hellfire" in a very different way. As already noted, until that is done, we cannot be sure we have found the truth of the matter.

Twists of the Human Mind

Some say it is God's love that moves Him to burn the lost. The wicked would not be happy in heaven, would disrupt the joy of the righteous. Therefore, some say God merely separates them into hell fire, burning them briefly or eternally, depending on who you talk to. This tidy solution fails to consider several factors; first, that Scripture clearly states, "the dead know not anything," that they are simply sleeping in the grave until resurrection morning (See Appendices B and C); second, that Scripture defines "forever" in *two* ways (to be discussed); and third, that God's character and the nature of death by burning are *mutually exclusive*. The God who gave His Son to die such a terrible death on Calvary *could not* then inflict agony upon His creatures at such a monstrous level as to burn them—eternally or otherwise.

A pastor friend once asked his congregation for a show of hands: "If you could choose the means by which you would lose your life, which would you choose: a knife, a bullet or burning. Not one chose burning. Why? It's hard to imagine a more painful death, not to mention burning for eternity. Yet we attribute to our Creator God the intention to burn His children who choose not to follow Him. And God, who is omnipotent, has choices in the means of executing this destruction. When we say God burns His own creatures, we say He *decides* to do it that way, that He has less humanity than we, because He can do such a deed and call it righteous. How can it be right when God does it and yet when humans do it, no punishment is deemed too harsh for their crime?

While many in Christendom accept this view of God without a wince, numerous others see through it. It cannot be true, they say, and so they invent the theory of macro-evolution, humanism, atheism, to replace a system of belief that violates their reason, and they are lost to the gospel. Does God really love the world so much He gave His only Son that it might not *perish*? If He can turn right around and burn His children who fail to receive the Gift, then giving His Son to die couldn't have been such a sacrifice in His mind. How callous He appears in this picture!

If the church is to connect with the minds of many thinking people in this world, it must address this bizarre, unrealistic presentation of God. Any theologian worth his or her salary, analyzing the situation, would see that something doesn't add up and would desire a closer look.

The Love of the Inquisitors

The "Inquisition" occurred during the darkest of the dark ages. It was a time when conventional wisdom held the church to have ecclesiastical authority over the human conscience. Thus she consigned "heretics" to the rack and other assorted implements of torture to reclaim them, as the inquisitors viewed it, for God's kingdom. Failing in this, the flames of the *auto de fe* sufficed to speed them on their way to eternal torment.

Do you know they did it out of love? If they could "inspire" a heretic to recant, they would save his soul, so they thought. Thus they were really doing him a favor by torturing him. If he failed to recant, burning would be his fate anyway. Thus, burning him at the stake made good sense to them.

Where did this grisly idea begin? It originated in their view of God. One's picture of God, accepted as truth, can justify the strangest thinking. Does reason not dictate that some things are right and some things are wrong, regardless of whether done by "god" or by humans—regardless of whatever righteous claim the tormentors make?

Fire From the Sky

Revelation 20:9 contains the clearest and most succinct statement in Scripture of the final execution of the wicked: "Fire came down from God out of heaven and devoured them [the lost]."

This quotation appears in some Greek manuscripts and modern translations as "Fire came down out of heaven and devoured them," deleting reference to God as the agent. Does the fire originate with God or simply drop from the sky in some way without God's intervening to prevent it? By now we may suspect the latter to be the case.

In answering these questions it will be helpful to first examine Scriptural incidents of "fire from the sky."

1. The first record of fire from the sky occurred during Job's great test. God had released Job's possessions into Satan's power with resultant loss, first, of his livestock and then of his children, seemingly in a moment of time. One message the beleaguered man received was, "The fire of God fell from heaven and burned up the sheep and the servants." But whose fire was it really? Again, God got "credit" for something He only allowed. (See Job 1:16.)

2. Fire next descended, according to Scripture, in connection with the plague of hail in Egypt. We have examined evidence supporting the view that Satan was the destroyer of Egypt's firstborn and that God "gave their life over to the plague," strongly suggesting He lost authority over various aspects of nature, releasing them into Satan's power. We therefore have reason to suspect that Satan also officiated both over the plague of hail and the fire connected with it. (See Exodus 9:24.)

3. "Fire went out from the Lord" and burned up Nadab and Abihu, sons of Aaron. (See Leviticus 10:1,2.)

4. A fire consumed 250 Hebrew princes involved in the Korah rebellion. We have already established that, during this episode, lives lost for complaining (and these certainly qualify) were attributable to the destroyer (Satan). (p.73; see 1 Corinthians 10:10.)

5. The next incident occurred when David offered sacrifice and called on the Lord, "and He answered him from heaven by fire on the altar of burnt offering." (See 1 Chronicles 21:26.)

6. Upon completion of Solomon's temple, Israel's second permanent center of worship, fire from heaven fell and consumed the prepared sacrifices. (See 2 Chronicles 7:1.)

7. Fire fell from heaven and consumed Elijah's sacrifice, denoting him as heaven's prophet. (See 1 Kings 18:38.)

8. On two occasions in response to the prophet Elijah's decree, fire from heaven burned up companies of fifty-one men each (2 Kings 1:9-12). To human vision God seems to have executed these men personally. But we know from the story of Job and other sources that God only releases humans into the power of Satan and natural disasters. God could certainly communicate to His prophet the means by which the destroyer would execute these men, since He Himself had released that means into the destroyer's power. Keep in mind how committed Israel was, under Ahab, to a policy of sin and separation from God. The possibility these men may have forfeited God's protection cannot be ignored. Satan, ever vigilant to blame God for human suffering, has nothing to lose by executing his own at such times.[30]

9. Revelation 13:13 predicts a time yet future when fire will again fall from heaven. The context is clear that Satan or his agent, still playing God, brings it as a means to deceive the world into worshiping him.

Apparently, either God or Satan can bring fire from the sky, just as both turned staffs into snakes in Pharaoh's Egypt (Exodus 7:10-12). Even if God says He does it, we cannot tell from that alone if He does it in the traditional sense, as you or I would do a thing, or whether He simply permits it to happen.

Spirits of Devils, Working Miracles

How, then, can we know the source of these and other "miracles"? "To the law and to the testimony! If they do not speak according to this word [the Bible], it is because there is no light in them" (Isaiah 8:20). That beleaguered old Volume, set aside by the world, God still calls the antidote to deception and the guidepost to eternal life.

It tells how God feels about igniting humans with fire from the sky. The Samaritans, traditional rivals of Israel, slighted Jesus by refusing hospitality to Him and His disciples. John and James were indignant. "Shall we command fire from heaven to consume them, as Elijah did?" they ask.

Their question reflects not only an absence of common mercy but also a grave misunderstanding of God's character. Because they understood that He endorsed such things, they lost touch with the horribleness of it—a common

---

[30]Note the similarity between Nos. 4 and 8 above, in that the prophet in each case predicts the destruction [in Moses' case, an earthquake; in Elijah's, fire from heaven] as *proof of his prophetic calling*. Yet Christ *denies* participation in the Elijah episode, involving destruction of two companies of soldiers by fire (Luke 9:55, 56; John 3:16, 17). Nor, by implication, was He the agent of Korah's death.

occurrence in traditional church thinking, where "Christians" sometimes do strange and terrible things fully confident they are fulfilling the will of God. Can you picture the look on Jesus' face at this monstrous suggestion? He gently reproves them, "You do not know *what manner of spirit* you are of. For the Son of Man did not come to destroy men's lives but to save them" (Luke 9:55,56).

On the basis of His reply we may conclude that God may send fire from heaven to consume a sacrifice but not to consume humans. The idea is, in fact, repugnant to Him, *the work of another spirit.*

The Source of Final Fire

That fire, then, comes from the sky and consumes the unsaved. *But God does not send it.* From where, then, does it come? God speaks:

> I brought fire *from your midst*;
>> It devoured you,
>>> And I turned you to ashes upon the earth
>>> In the sight of all who saw you.(Ezekiel 28:18)

Ezekiel 28 contains one of the primary descriptions in Scripture of Lucifer, later known as Satan. Analyzing the above from that chapter gives us this:

"I" — God, indicating His *permitted* will, describes Himself as doing what He only allows. This says He could have prevented this experience but chose not to intervene.

"Fire" — The fire from the sky of Revelation 20:9

"Your" — Lucifer's/ Satan's

"From your midst" — Somehow Satan is responsible for creating the mechanism of his own fiery destruction, thus confirming the self-destructive nature of sin.

"Turned you to ashes" — Indicates *annihilation.* More on this later.

Where Does Hell Occur—and How Long?

Scripture indicates that the final fire comes from Satan in some way. But would he burn himself up? Hold that question. We'll come back to it. First some details of that final fire. As to its location, some are surprised to learn it takes place on this earth. "If the righteous will be recompensed [rewarded] on the earth, how much more the wicked and the sinner" (Proverbs 11:31).

Before this earth becomes the eternal home of the saved, it will be the scene of the fiery blotting out of the lost.

As to the duration of that fire, Christians, in the tradition of Jonathan Edwards, have handed down a concept that sinners burn eternally. And many Christians will not entertain any inquiry into the validity of that belief. A minister, in fact, declared he would not even be a Christian were he not convinced that sinners burn endlessly. Many diligently protect this belief, using it as an evangelistic tool. Yet this same belief has probably created as many atheists as Christians. No harm can come from examining and clarifying this doctrine.

Yes, sinners do perish. Scripture is clear on that. Humans do not escape the wages of sin, except through the cross of Christ, by repentance and a close personal walk with God. But would *eternal* burning be *just* for the sins of one short lifetime? And is God just? Of course He is. Justice, remember, is not vindictiveness. It is not a license to torture. To be just, the punishment must fit the crime. God was just, when He released His Son, in the role of the Sin-bearer, to His fate, but nowhere does Scripture even suggest that it was eternal burning.

Believers in a place where the lost burn eternally have the difficult task of showing how Christ experienced that fate, for if it is truly the fate of the lost and Christ did *not* experience it, then we are without a Savior and yet in our sins. Do you see the problems embodied in that idea?

Two Perspectives

The need to focus the topic prevents full coverage of the question of how long the lost burn. Other authors have devoted full books to it. For now we shall limit ourselves to a few representative quotations. Here are some that seem to support the idea of an eternally burning hell.

- Depart from Me, you cursed, into the everlasting fire prepared for the devil and his angels (Matthew 25:41).

- They will be tormented day and night forever and ever (Revelation 20:10).

- Its smoke shall ascend forever (Isaiah 34:10).

In contrast, many references state that Satan will be ashes (Ezekiel 28:18), that he will one day be no more forever (Ezekiel 28:19); the wicked will be ashes (Malachi 4:3); the fire will devour or totally consume them (Revelation 20:9), and many more, thus . . .

How Long Will the Wicked Suffer Final Punishment?

One Perspective	Another Perspective
They will be tormented day and night *forever and ever* (Revelation 20:10)	The day which is coming shall *burn them up . . . they shall be ashes* (Malachi 4:1, 2).

The Bible record of Sodom and Gomorrah holds the key to this contradiction. Remember, God warned His people through the prophets that they were repeating the history of those cities and would therefore share their fate, which turned out to be *abandonment.* He also holds Sodom and Gomorrah up to us today as examples of the duration of that final fire.

How Long Did Sodom and Gomorrah Burn?

One Perspective	Another Perspective
As Sodom and Gomorrah . . . are set forth as an example, suffering the vengeance of *eternal* fire (Jude 7).	And turning the cities of Sodom and Gomorrah into *ashes* (2 Peter 2:6).

If we had only these references, they would be enough, for look as we may we will find no cities of the Middle East burning since antiquity. The fire which consumed those cities obviously *burned them up and died out*,[31] but why would Scripture describe them as burning eternally? And why would numerous Bible writers depict the final fire as "eternal," if it, in fact, burns out?

A final reference clarifies what "eternal" or "forever" *can* mean Biblically. "[A slave's] master shall also bring him to the . . . door. . . and he shall serve him *forever*" (Exodus 20:6;). Here "forever" means until death. That is "forever" to the slave. Only death can end forever. Only a world where death is unknown can enjoy a forever without end. To those unwise enough to take part in the final fire, forever or eternity ends for them at their last breath.

"For God so loved the world that He gave His only begotten Son, that whoever believes in Him should not *perish* . . . " (John 3:16). Think about that word, "perish." Look it up in the dictionary. In concluding that the fiery fate of the wicked burns on throughout eternity, have we considered the meaning of the word "perish"? There is no evidence in Scripture of the word "perish" meaning anything other than complete and final annihilation. Christ died to relieve humans of that fate.

However, the word "forever" *may* be literal or symbolic Scripturally, depending upon the context. We use the term "forever" symbolically to

---

[31]You will find the same pattern in connection with the "unquenchable" fire that destroyed Jerusalem anciently (See Jeremiah 17:27 and 2 Chronicles 36:19-21). "Unquenchable" fire is simply fire that cannot be quenched by human effort. It does not mean God miraculously perpetuates it.

denote a seemingly unending period; for example, we might say, I waited *forever* in line at the bank.

Another reason may exist for the sense of the everlasting so common in descriptions of that final fire—a reason which detracts not at all from the above logic. The tendency of the prophets to depict it as "everlasting," "eternal," and "forever" suggests that if you or I, as they did, could look out upon that molten sea of boiling orange stretched to the horizon and beyond in all directions, no power but that of God able to quench it until its cleansing work is done, in a transport of panic we too might cry out, "The smoke of their torment ascends forever and ever" (Revelation 14:11). Truly it must have seemed that way to the prophets who saw it in holy vision.

The Judgments of God

The judgments of God we have addressed thus far—the flood, Sodom and Gomorrah, the plagues of Egypt, etc.—already existed within the environment, awaiting withdrawal of God's protecting power to perform their destructive work. To fit the same pattern and follow the same principles, potential for the final fiery destruction must exist within the human environment of earth's last days. It should in some way come from the sky and be a self-evident product of the mind of one who can only and most accurately be termed "the destroyer."

Not that Satan would deliberately immerse himself in a lake of fire. But could it happen by accident, as the final episode of sin's inherent "boomerang effect?" "The indignation of the Lord is against all nations, and His fury against all their armies; He has utterly destroyed them; He has *given them over* to the slaughter" (Isaiah 34:2;).

More Biblical information exists regarding this terrible disaster; however, further study would first require a background on Armageddon, judgment, resurrection—digressions too extensive to incorporate into this small work.

It is sufficient to know that the Bible concludes this macabre episode on a positive note, as God overrules Satan's final destructive act and turns it into good. "A fire devours before them [observers] and behind them a flame burns; the land is like the Garden of Eden before them, and behind them a desolate wilderness" (Joel 2:3).

That fire, monument to Lucifer and his arrogant claims against God, serves at last a noble purpose. Sin, sinners, root and branch, with all the evidence thereof, will vanish in those flames, which, dying out, disclose a blackened earth, awaiting God's command to restore the original creation(Malachi 4:1, 3; Revelation 21:1-4).

13

LIFE ONLY IN CHRIST

"The thief cometh not, but for to steal, and to kill, and to destroy: I am come that they might have life, and that they might have it more abundantly" (John 10:10).

We start asking the question in childhood: Why didn't God just destroy Lucifer and prevent the disaster the world is in? The answer? God wanted to be served out of love rather than fear. If God executes the opposition, He would have an orderly world, all right. But something would be missing, something important to God and to us: our freedom. And the respect and honor, which alone can move our hearts to worship Him.

No amount of time or intervening events cancels this truth. If God could not deny Lucifer's free will, then He must extend the same freedom to all His intelligent creation.

Loyalty to God has no value in the absence of free will. From eternity past the intelligences of God's creation have had an option which God would preserve even in view of the emergency conditions existing when sin entered His domain. He met the crisis not by killing off the opposition. He had another idea—the cross of His own dear Son. That cross has drawing power over thinking minds. It wins their loyalty. It inspires a free-will desire to obey Him, and it makes a statement about God by which to measure all theories about the character of Deity.

Having resolved from eternity past to pay such a price to secure His creatures' life and freedom, in the interests of consistency He could not then personally execute the surface-thinkers who failed to value the gift.

We have interpreted the Bible's abundant warnings against sin as saying "God will get you," rather than hearing the true message, that sin contains the seeds of its own destruction. It separates from God, the one Source of life and protection and sustenance in the universe.

A respected pastor shared this thought with me: "I have tried to illustrate this to people by the analogy of a parent who knows that her or his child is in a burning house and just stands there watching it burn without any attempt to rescue the one inside. In actual fact, it would take probably five firemen to hold such a parent back under these circumstances when it is clear that it would be suicide to try a rescue. All of God's instincts demand that He move to the saving of any of His creatures who are in trouble, but the time will come when He is held back from doing this simply because they have beaten Him out of their lives."

Union With Christ

The theme of union with Christ, while familiar to Christians, may come as a new thought to others, who may yet desire to know more about this thing called oneness with the invisible God.

No Scriptural concept is more emphasized than this. Through many and varied symbols God has told us of His desire for union with His people. Jesus spoke of hens and chicks, of partaking of His flesh and blood. The temple, for generations the focus of the nation's religion, symbolized a God in the midst of Israel (Deuteronomy 30:11-14; Romans 10:5-8).

A lowly desert shrub became holy in the only way possible for shrubs or humans to become holy—by Divine presence. God told Moses, and later, Joshua, "Take your sandal off your foot, for the place where you stand is holy" (Exodus 3:5; Joshua 5:15). Again, it was the presence of Deity that made it so. Humans may aspire to holiness only through living in the presence of a holy God.

But here again, we must think in opposites in order to understand. Human eligibility for salvation hinges upon acknowledging our own sinfulness. When we see the high standard of God and believe we can reach it, we haven't looked high enough yet. The holiness of God is totally beyond human grasp.

The parable of the Pharisee and the sinner who went up to the temple to pray, illustrates this truth. The Pharisee thought himself securely in God's grace, but the other prayed, "God be merciful to me a sinner!" (Luke 18:13). These words were not part of a religious ritual but the expression of a man overwhelmed by his own capacity to sin. He smote upon his breast, could not so much as lift his eyes to God. He wanted God's forgiveness, but if it depended upon his being good, it was beyond him. He had no option but to throw himself upon heaven's mercy. "This man went down to his house justified," accepted of God (v. 14).

When the prophet Isaiah caught a glimpse of the holiness of God, it cast his human pride into the dust. "Woe is me," he said, "for I am undone!" (Isaiah 6:5). Laodicea, proud Laodicea, fails to see her "wretched, miserable, poor, blind, and naked" condition (Revelation 3:17) and thus her soul is at risk, because only those who see their lost condition feel the need of a Redeemer outside themselves.

But rather than allowing the inescapable fact of their sinful nature to torment and destroy them, they take their helplessness to Jesus and day by day make *His* beautiful character their meditation. Gradually and not without struggle against their human frailties, the vision transforms them (2 Corinthians 3:18), until His character is formed within. And when the work is done, they are the very last to know it, for never this side of heaven will humans dare trust in their own inherent strength to do the right. Never, in this life, must humans lose sight of their vulnerability to sin. Just as recovering alcoholics say, "I am an alcoholic," even though they do not drink, until eternity the child of God says, "I am a sinner," but through God's grace puts the sin away. It is this awareness of vulnerability to sin, free moral agency connected with fallen human nature, that brings the child of God to the foot of the cross day by day and moment by moment to yield the life over to One who, through His Spirit, brings the victory.

Symbols of God's Presence

How assuring it is to know that Christ came to call, not those who deem themselves righteous, but those who deem themselves sinners to repent and live in His enabling, ennobling presence (Matthew 9:13). And walking day-by-day in that Divine presence, and unbeknownst to themselves, Christ imparts to them the beauty of His own righteous character.

The symbols of light and water recur in Scripture as representing God's presence. How better could He convey the omnipresence of His Spirit than in Christ's words, "I am the Light of the world" (John 8:12). How better could He describe a world without His Spirit than as a kingdom full of darkness (Revelation 16:10). "God is light," says the apostle John, "and in Him is *no darkness at all*" (1 John 1:5).

To the woman at Jacob's well He offered living water. And on an ancient Passover, He stood and cried out, "If anyone thirsts, let him come to Me and drink. He who believes in Me, as the Scripture has said, out of his heart will flow rivers of living water" (John 7:37, 38).

Water in particular came to have special meaning as the door to the infant church. Jesus said to Nicodemus, "Unless one is born of water and the Spirit, he cannot enter the kingdom of God" (John 3:5). Jesus said He was the door (John 10:7). But converts also pass through baptismal waters on the way into the church, the body of Christ. That too is the door. If the waters symbolize Christ's presence through the Holy Spirit, one could imagine an event unseen to human eyes occurring when humans enter and then leave the baptismal water. They enter alone, but they leave clad in an invisible robe represented by the water, walking with an invisible Presence. No longer alone, they enjoy an abiding fellowship with Christ to whom they give pre-eminence. His glory becomes their reason for being.

The robe figures largely in the catalog of Biblical symbols. Jesus told a story about a man who came to a wedding feast without one. It wasn't that he had no robe. The host had, in fact, provided all the guests, including him, with robes. But this man chose to come in common garments, and when asked why, he had nothing to say. "Cast him out," said the host. He could not attend the wedding feast, representing the "wedding supper of the Lamb" without that stainless garment (Matthew 22:1-14; Revelation 19:9).

Communion

If we are to know Christ's presence, we must learn to commune with Him. Words are the bonds in this relationship. He speaks to us through His word. We give Him our gratitude, praise, joys, needs, burdens, always in words. We learn to claim His word for our needs, to assume His presence and His mercy. We speak "to" Him more than "of" Him. We make Him first in our lives, and thus we abide in Him and bear fruit (actions and attitudes) in harmony with the kingdom of God. We are accepted only in Him—"in the Beloved" (Ephesians 1:6), as He draws over us the covering of His Spirit (Isaiah 30:1, KJV).

Many even in the church do not live in this fellowship with their Lord. They may observe the ritual vigorously, but they have no sweet Lord to empower them and lift them above the strife of human passions. They have no peace nor joy.

If your experience fits this description or if you have never accepted Christ into your life at all, why not this very moment decide to open the door of your heart and let Him in? He's been there knocking ever so long. Don't delay longer. Let Him in. Say, "Come in, Lord Jesus. Abide with me today. I accept You as King and Lord of my life."

Read His word and give Him your words every morning. Never leave your prayer closet without humbly insisting in Jesus' name that He come with you and be Captain of your day. Pour out everything in your heart at that moment. Never forget to praise Him. Thank Him for the armor of God and strap it on. Ask Him to sit upon the throne of your soul; give Him all the powers of your being—your seeing (ask for heavenly eyesalve; Revelation 3:18), your hearing (ask to hear His still small voice and for power quickly to obey; 1 Kings, 19:12), your speaking (ask Him to touch your lips with a coal from off the altar and purge your sin, for the power to speak a word in season to one who is weary; Isaiah 6:6,7; 50:4). The word of God is full of precious things we may have if we only ask.

"Christ In You, The Hope of Glory"

But the character is all His. All the fruits reside in Him and flow to His children through that abiding relationship. Love, joy, peace, longsuffering, kindness, goodness, faithfulness, gentleness, self-control characterize the life in which the Holy Spirit reigns (Galatians 5:22, 23).[32] His moral law ceases to condemn, as that abiding communion provides the power joyfully to obey, evidencing His presence. Of those who have discovered this powerful relationship Scripture says, "Here are those who keep the commandments of God and [or through] the faith of Jesus" (Revelation 14:12), or Jesus living out His faith in the believer. His is the power, and to Him belongs the glory! "For as many of you as were baptized into Christ *have put on Christ*" (Galatians 3:27;).

The Bible depicts this union between the Holy Spirit and humans as the ideal toward which God calls us. He does the wooing. He provided the cross. We make the choice. God calls earnestly to the vast unnumbered masses of uncommitted humanity upon this earth to surrender to His sovereignty and live. Through various avenues He appeals to us to give up our destructive toys, attitudes, methods, ways . . . and live.

Christ did His part on Calvary's cross. He provided a perfect sacrifice. Its completeness more than reaches the depth of all our sin. He longs to be At-One with His creation but now awaits that moment when our understanding of Him deepens and draws us to make that choice to follow Him. The free will He gives us He will never compromise.

The Bible predicts that immediately prior to Christ's return everyone will have made a choice for God or for His enemy. The latter is the default. "*All* who dwell upon the earth will worship him [Satan] whose names have not been written in the Book of Life of the Lamb slain from the foundation of the world" (Revelation 13:8;). At that time God declares, "Babylon the great [man-made religion] is fallen, is fallen, and has become a habitation of demons" (Revelation 18:2). The choice, then, is whether we shall be God-possessed by the Holy Spirit or demon possessed in the enemy's camp, for the great uncommitted body of humanity shall have vanished in a flurry of final choices.

How strange that we could ever think God could dismiss compassion. He could as easily stop being God. Christ portrayed His Father's heart when, on Olivet's brow, surrounded by a multitude of rejoicing admirers intent on His coronation, His heart sobbed "like a flute" for a lost people. His sorrow broke forth in sudden dissonance, like a wailing in a hallelujah chorus. In

---

[32]To these I daily add petitions for wisdom and good judgment, courage and power, energy and productivity, truth and honesty, health and strength.

that glad scene of celebration, Israel's King poured out tears of inexpressible woe, because He saw the lost condition of a people who "knew not the time of their visitation."

"Oh, Jerusalem, Jerusalem! . . . How often I wanted to gather your children together, as a hen gathers her chicks under her wings, but you were not willing!"

The pathos sounds down the centuries to our time. "Oh, world, world! careless, indifferent, preoccupied world! How often I wanted to gather you, to shield you from the day of wrath appointed unto you, but you would not."

And over the dark and secret places of our world; in seemingly impregnable corridors of power; through the restless cadence of a thousand rushing cities broods a faintly haunting, melancholy whisper from the past. "Ephraim is joined to idols. Let him alone" (Hosea 4:17).

A Biblical Sampler

> ## FORMULA CODE
> [Because sin is chosen]   *Results in trouble*
> **God withdraws**   /Equals His wrath/

NOTE: Emphasis is underlined

1.   But You, O Lord, **do not be far from Me**; O My Strength, hasten to help me. . . . For He has not despised nor abhorred the *affliction of the afflicted*; Nor has He **hidden His face** from Him: But when He cried to Him, He heard (Psalm 22:19, 24).

2.   Why do you **stand afar off**, O Lord? Why do You **hide Yourself** in times of *trouble*? (Psalm 10:1).

3.   Do not **hide Your face** from me; Do not turn Your servant away in /anger/ (Psalm 27:9).

4.   How long, Lord? Will You **hide Yourself** forever? Will Your /wrath/ burn like fire? (Psalm 89:46).

5.   Do not **hide Your face** from me, lest I be like those who go down into the *pit* (Psalm 143:7).

6.   Your New Moons and your appointed feasts My soul hates; they are a trouble to Me; I am weary of bearing them. When you spread out your hands, I will **hide My eyes** from you; even though you make many prayers, I will not hear. [Your hands are full of blood] (Isaiah 1:15).

7.   Behold I will gather them out of all countries where I have driven them in My /anger/, in My /fury/, and in great /wrath/ . . . I will not **turn away** from doing them good (Jeremiah 32:27, 40).

[**NOTE:** The following reference explains more fully that the hiding of God's face refers to the removal of His Holy Spirit.]

8.   "And I will not **hide My face** from them anymore; for I shall have poured out My Spirit on the house of Israel," says the Lord God (Ezekiel 39:29).

9.   **I will return again to My place** till they acknowledge their [offense]. Then they will seek My face; in their *affliction* they will diligently seek Me (Hosea 5:15).

10.   *Woe* to them when I **depart** from them! (Hosea 9:12).

11.   The Lord was like an enemy.
He has *swallowed up* Israel
            He has *swallowed up* all her palaces;
                  He has *destroyed* her strongholds,
And increased *mourning and lamentation*
In the daughter of Judah.
            He has done violence to His tabernacle,
                  As if it were a garden;
He has *destroyed* His place of assembly;
            The Lord has caused
                  The appointed feasts and Sabbaths
                        to be forgotten in Zion.
In His burning /indignation/ ["Wrath," JB]
            He has **spurned** the king and the priest.
                  The Lord has **spurned** His altar;
                        He has **abandoned** His sanctuary;
He has **given up** the walls of her palaces
                        into the hand of the enemy.
                              (Lamentations 2:5-7)

12.   "You have feared the sword; and *I will bring a sword upon you*," says the Lord God. "And I will bring you out of its midst and *deliver you into the hands of strangers*, and *execute judgments on you*" (Ezekiel 11:8,9).

13.   His master was /angry/, and **delivered him** to the torturers until he should pay all that was due to him. **So My heavenly Father also will do to you** if each of you, from his heart, does not forgive his brother his trespasses (Matthew 18:34, 35).

14.   He who strikes a man so that he dies shall surely be put to death. But if he did not lie in wait, but **God delivered him into his hand**,

then I will appoint for you a place where he may flee (Exodus 21:12, 13. This refers to the Cities of Refuge, symbols of Christ).

15.   Because you have <u>forsaken</u> the Lord, He also has **forsaken** you (2 Chronicles 24:20).

16.   **Those who are far from you shall perish.**
> You have *destroyed* all those
>> who <u>desert</u> you for harlotry.
> But it is good for me to draw near to God.
>> (Psalm 73:27, 28).

17.   You shall no longer be termed forsaken . . . You shall be called Sought Out, a city not forsaken (Isaiah 62:4, 12).

18.   "Go, take yourself a wife of harlotry" (Hosea 1:2). Would God, in fact, direct His prophet to "take . . . a wife of harlotry"? While clearly depicting the relationship between God and his apostate people, this choice of a life's companion brought the prophet only heartache. Ever after, Bible students have wondered over these strange words of God to the prophet Hosea. Why would God inflict this disaster on His servant?

After more than two millennia, insights from the message of God's loving character may finally have solved this riddle.

Note the similarity between God's words to Hosea and His words to Moses:"[Go], send men to spy out the land of Canaan" (Numbers 13:2).

But in describing the incident to the Israelites 40 years later, Moses said,"Everyone of *you* came near to me and said, 'Let us send men before us, and let them search out the land for us'" (Deuteronomy 1:22). The idea to spy out the land clearly originated with the people themselves; God merely gave permission. He Himself did not need to spy out the land; He knew what was there.

Comparing the "spying" incident to God's strange command to Hosea suggests the prophet may have become smitten with Gomer, asked God if he could marry her, and the first words of Scripture describing the matter are God's, verbalizing His permission—along with His warning of the outcome of the match.

The context shows Hosea's profound emotional attachment to Gomer, a strong connection that would be difficult to command, even for Deity. Again, God overrules this disastrous bonding by using it to show His own deep emotional yearnings over His wayward people.

APPENDIX B

Where Did Jesus Go When He Died?[33]

"The hail shall sweep away
the refuge of lies"
(Isaiah 28:17)

The evangelist stood at the lectern, pleading with the overflow crowd assembled before him in the huge auditorium, to surrender to the claims of the cross and come to God. He reached forth in entreaty; his voice rose with fervor, as he implored his listeners to cease resisting the promptings of the Holy Spirit, to stop rebelling against heaven, and to yield to the love of the One who died on Calvary's cross to redeem them.

"You will spend eternity somewhere," he said. "*You* choose where you will spend it, in heaven or in the realms of the lost." He couldn't seem to bring himself to utter the words, in the fires of the damned. Nonetheless, the message was clear. "Turn or burn." Respond to the love of God, or this loving God will burn you eternally. And it will be *your* fault, not His.

Throughout the cavernous assembly hall, listeners, moved by his oratory, stood to their feet and began stepping out into the isles. Quickly the lines thickened and lengthened, until a great sea of humanity, stretching far back toward the auditorium's darkened lobby, eagerly made its way down the wide stairs and toward the altar in front. Handkerchiefs and tissues flew from pockets and purses, as tears streamed down the faces of both those newly coming to Christ and those who had perhaps prayed for this day, when loved ones would take their stand for God. What was the deep motive moving the hearts of the people there that day? Did they commit because the love of Christ constrained them? Or to escape an eternity of the tortures of the damned?

To all appearances it was a great day of victory for the gospel. But appearances can deceive. True, a multitude of people received Christ on

---

[33]This appendix was intended for use as a chapter of the book. However, a place could not be found to insert it where it did not interrupt the flow of thought. Yet in order to see God as nondestructive, it is so important to understand the human condition in death that it is included here as an appendix.

that day. But how many *more* have turned away from Christ, turned off to God, because Christendom has not yet resolved its disquieting questions, those questions which well-intentioned advocates of the gospel, such as the evangelist that day, continue to ignore? Compare the crowd in that auditorium with the untold millions throughout time who cannot relate to God, as Christianity presents Him.

The theory seems to be, If the version of the gospel which depicts God as all-loving on one hand and utterly cruel and vengeful on the other still has power to gain some adherents, that's good enough for us. We will continue to present Him in that way in spite of the fact that in many ways it doesn't make sense, and it turns more people *off* than on. It says Christianity's God does not have the mature, integrated, consistent character expected of even well-adjusted humans.

"The path of the just is as a shining sun [footnote: "light"] that shines ever brighter unto the perfect day" (Proverbs 4:18). Where is that expanding ray of light? Where is the heightened illumination on those issues that honest men and women, in and out of the church, have questioned from time immemorial? In actual fact, Scripture offers very clear answers to these questions, and they begin to be answered in the Person of the uplifted Christ, hanging upon the cross for the sins of the world.

"Jesus, when He had cried out again with a loud voice, yielded up His spirit" (Matt. 27:50. See also Luke 23:46 and John 19:30). Where did Jesus go when He died? In order to be correctly understood, every truth of God's word must be studied in the light that streamed from His cross that day. Just as Christ experienced life as a human, He shared our human experience in death. In fact, His death was the *sinner's* death. The brazen serpent Moses lifted up in the wilderness represented Christ, the Sin-bearer. Did Christ's spirit leave His body at death and go to a place of eternal torment?

So much about our understanding of God revolves around this question. Everything depends upon *the example Christ gave* of how God deals with the lost. The truth about death as it applied to Christ is key to understanding the Lifegiver's character.

The Surprising Biblical Picture of Death

A talented and well-known singer/actress, speaking on a television talk show, expressed a view commonly held today. She stated she believed in "life after life", not "life after death." In other words, she and multitudes of others, do not believe death is really death at all. Representing the majority view, this lady spoke of someone she knew who had "made his transition."

Within virtually every philosophy known among humans today, including Christianity, the belief exists that death is not death at all but a transition to a different form of life. In few places other than the pages of the Holy Bible do we find death depicted according to the dictionary definition as, *"permanent ending of all life in a person, animal or plant."* That's what death is, folks, and no amount of tweaking the perception can change the reality.

In order to convey a clear picture of how God destroys, it is necessary to visit the controversial topic of what death is in the first place. Without correct knowledge regarding the nature of death, it is *impossible* to understand God's role in it, so closely tied are these two elements of truth, so firmly does truth on one point become the foundation for higher truth.

Keep in mind, we are using the Holy Bible as our text and guide for the entire journey. Therefore, we must search Scripture for information on death, in order to understand, as well, God's character. We may have confidence regarding the nature of death on the authority of the following words of our Lord Jesus Christ:

"I have come *that they may have life*" (John 10:10).

If everyone already has life by virtue of an indestructible "spirit" or "soul" that goes somewhere when the body dies, why would Jesus say this? No, he does not say, I came to give *the body* life. Rather, He came *in order that* humans may live beyond the grave. Although this flies in the face of the beliefs of virtually everyone, although it contradicts the sensory experience of multitudes, although almost no one wants to believe it, yet it is the Bible picture. Death is the cessation of life. The atheist is right on this point, at least. Words mean what they appear to mean.

Obviously, the Bible has a great deal more to say about it. Here are just a few samples:

- For the living know that they will die; but the dead know nothing, and they have no more reward, for the memory of them is forgotten. Also their love, their hatred, and their envy have now perished; nevermore will they have a share in anything done under the sun. . . . Whatever your hand finds to do, do it with your might; for there is no work or device or knowledge or wisdom in the grave where you are going (Ecclesiastes 9:5, 6, 10).

- Jesus said, "'Our friend Lazarus sleeps, but I go that I may wake him up.' Then His disciples said, 'Lord, if he sleeps he will get well.' However, Jesus spoke of his death. . . . Then Jesus said to them plainly, 'Lazarus is dead'" (John 11:11). [**Note:** Death is like unconscious sleep.]

- In death there is no remembrance of You; In the grave who will give You thanks (Psalm 6:5). [**Note:** The dead cannot remember God or give Him thanks.]

- Trust not in princes—in a son of man, for he hath no deliverance. His spirit ["breath", James 2:26, KJV, margin] goeth forth, he returneth to his earth, in that day have his thoughts perished [(Psalm 146:3,4, YLT) **Note:** The "spirit" sometimes spoken of as leaving the body at death is simply the God-given breath, which enables the body to live and *symbolizes* the life or personality. Don't miss the point that *on the day of death, the thoughts perish.*]

These quotations constitute only a small portion of what Scripture has to say on this subject, supporting the view that death is the cessation of life. Others have written comprehensively on the topic of death, and you will find reviews and bibliographies of some of them in Appendix C. Thoughtful men and women who sincerely seek truth, like careful shoppers, examine the range of choices before making their selection. Sweeping back the layers of theological "goods" that have virtually erased the idea that death is "soul sleep" (as some call it), we uncover a centuries-old (though minority) view known within theological circles as "conditional immortality."

When the "Dead" Appear

No doubt many readers are asking at this point, but what about … ? Yes, what about all those *experiences*? A ghostly figure was seen which looked exactly like old uncle Ned. Footsteps were heard; voices from an antechamber….

Besides Christianity's belief in heaven and hell, other religions offer alternate views of what lies "on the other side." A well-known journalist and television personality says she believes totally in reincarnation. She knows it's true, because it has been scientifically researched, and all those people couldn't be lying.

The evidence is almost overwhelming that there is something out there. Channelers convey information purported as coming from ancient Tibetan masters before or after their death. The evidence is *so convincing* to the human mind. We cannot fathom how these things could occur, unless they come from those who have "made their transition" and now seek to contact the world of the living.

Christianity itself, abandoning its tether in the word of God (on this and other points) joins right in, preaching the deceased straight to the rainbow-circled throne on high. Have you ever noticed how few are, conversely, preached straight into the eternal hell fires of damnation, regardless of the tone of their moral life on earth? No. That's not considered good form toward the bereaved. But let no mistake be made, in Christianity's view, if the righteous go directly to their eternal heavenly reward, there must be a hell for the souls who "didn't make it."

Eternal hell fire. What a fine piece of work this would be coming from the hand of an infinitely loving God! It doesn't make sense. And believe me, every piece of Scripture you can produce to *prove* it's true, I can put within *my* model where it looks quite different and *does* make perfect sense. God never asks us to leave our reason behind in order to understand His word.

Conditional Immortality

"Natural immortality" says that a spirit or soul, the essence of the individual, goes somewhere the moment of death. "Conditional immortality" says No; death means cessation of life. Mainstream Christianity joins with pagan religions throughout time in believing "natural immortality." However, throughout history, including today, there have always been believers in conditional immortality.

I've been to some funerals. Not uncommonly, I'm sure, I've sat through services where the speaker presented thoughts with which I did not agree. But in deference to the memory of the deceased, I, like some of you perhaps, set my jaw a bit and kept my mouth closed. I've listened to preachers seeking to comfort the living, saying the deceased was at that moment enjoying the companionship of heavenly angels, of God, and of loved ones who've gone before.

Yet a Bible text runs through my mind at such times, "Behold I am coming quickly," Jesus says, "and *my reward is with me*" (Revelation 22: 12). This is the consistent statement of Scripture. Jesus brings reward at His second coming, which is yet future. Consider the following text:

> I do not want you to be ignorant, brethren, concerning those who have fallen asleep, lest you sorrow as others who have no hope.
>
> For we believe that Jesus died and rose again, even so God will bring with Him those who sleep in Jesus.
>
> For this we say to you by the word of the Lord, that we who are alive and remain until the coming of the Lord will by no means precede those who are asleep.
>
> For the Lord Himself will descend from heaven with a shout, with the voice of an archangel, and with the trumpet of God. And the dead in Christ will rise first.
>
> Then we who are alive and remain shall be caught up together with them in the clouds to meet the Lord in the air. And thus we shall always be with the Lord.
>
> Therefore *comfort one another with these words* (1 Thessalonians 4:13-18).

Can anyone fail to see that this is speaking of *resurrection of the righteous* at the second coming of Christ? With *these* words we are to comfort the grieving friends and relatives of those who have died. If the righteous are *already* in heaven, enjoying their reward, why not direct that they be comforted with *that* thought? And why resurrection? Certainly not merely to reclaim the body, because nothing corrupt will enter heaven; Christ returns to reclaim *the person* and the first "reward" is a new, incorruptible body (1 Corinthians 15:51-55). It is in *this* that the Christian takes hope. Eternal life only exists in God's kingdom of glory and is granted *on the conditions* laid out in the word of God. Resurrection solved the problem of the death of Christ our Lord. It was an event modern Christians find worthy of celebration. Why? Because when Jesus died on Calvary's cross, He ceased to exist. He did not, because He could not, go anywhere. Without resurrection, which is both figuratively and literally God's call, neither Christ nor humans can experience life beyond the grave.

A Biblical Litmus Test

If you find none of this convincing, Scripture contains a story that may yet give you pause. Eve stood before the Tree of Knowledge of Good and Evil. Satan, disguised as a serpent in the tree, responded to her statement. She said God had warned that if she ate the fruit of the tree she would die. "You will not surely die," said he. "For God knows that in the day you eat of it your eyes will be opened, and you will be like God, knowing good and evil" (Genesis 3:4,5).

God said they would die. Satan declared they would not only live but enter upon a higher plane of existence. Both could not be telling the truth. Who lied, God or Satan?

This story is confusing to millions, because popular culture and religion, including mainstream Christianity, have received and promoted the idea that death is not death at all but the doorway to a higher form of life. These believers in the natural immortality of the soul have to conclude that Satan told the truth here, and God lied!

But Scripture is clear, Satan is the father of lying; he invented it (John 8: 44). It is *impossible* for God to lie (Hebrews 6: 18). And all liars will have a part in that final "lake that burns with fire" (Revelation 21:8).

The entire dilemma resolves, if we conclude that God told the truth here, and Satan lied—a picture entirely consistent with the concept of *conditional* immortality. Death is death. At the close of life, life closes.

Resurrection and Judgment

In his thorough and wonderful book, *Daring To Differ: Adventures In Conditional Immortality*, the late Sidney Hatch, Th.M., a Baptist minister, makes this observation: "The Athenians listened to him [the apostle Paul] until he mentioned the resurrection of the dead. Then, we read, 'some mocked: and others said, We will hear thee again of this matter [Acts 17:32].'

"The Athenians believed in the immortality of the soul. Luke's account in the Book of Acts indicates that, to them, resurrection from the dead was ridiculous." "Herein lies the tragedy of much of today's preaching and evangelism. It uses the name of Christ to teach a doctrine of ancient pagan philosophy" (pp. 7, 13).[34] Notice, the idea of *resurrection* appears odd to one who believes that rewards are issued immediately upon death. In that scenario, resurrection serves no obvious purpose.

But no honest Christian, even casually familiar with the Bible, can deny the emphasis Scripture places on the doctrine of resurrection. Here are a few quotations, with comments on them, that show how problematic it is to try to blend natural immortality with the Scriptural picture of life after death, particularly in those areas concerning *resurrection* and the *timing of the judgment*.

> When the Son of man shall come in his glory, and all the holy angels with him, then shall he sit upon the throne of his glory; and before him shall be gathered all nations; and he shall separate them one from another, as a shepherd divideth his sheep from the goats; and he shall set the sheep on his right hand, but the goats on the left. Then shall the King say unto them on his right hand, Come, ye blessed of my Father, inherit the kingdom prepared for you from the foundation of the world (Matthew 25:31-34, KJV).

This clearly refers to judgment, when the sheep and goats, the saved and lost, will be separated. It occurs, according to the context, at the time of the second coming of Christ. How can this be true *and* also be true that individuals receive their reward at death? The world has not yet experienced the second coming of Christ in the glory predicted in Scripture. Therefore, is it fair to say that neither have the sheep and goats been separated? That neither saint nor sinner has yet received his or her reward?

> For we must all appear before the judgment seat of Christ that every one may receive the things done in his body, according to that he hath done, whether it be good or bad (2 Corinthians 5:10).

This text agrees with Christ's words in Matthew 25. Scripture offers a consistent statement regarding judgment, as it does all other doctrines,

---

[34]Published by Brief Bible Studies, 21800 SW Pacific Hwy, #41, Sherwood, Oregon 97140-9130 ($9.95 plus $3 s/h). Highly readable and highly recommended to anyone wishing to explore this topic further.

when humans care enough to search them out. Humans receive reward at judgment, which takes place when Christ returns at the end of the world.

- All who are in the graves will hear His voice and come forth—those who have done good, to the resurrection of life, and those who have done evil, to the resurrection of condemnation (John 5:28, 29).

- Blessed and holy is he that hath part in the first resurrection; on such the second death hath no power (Revelation 20:6).

- The rest of the dead lived not again until the thousand years were finished (Revelation 20:5).

Close attention to the above references reveals there will be two resurrections, one of the righteous and another of the unrighteous. Nothing here suggests an eternally-burning hell for the wicked or immediate entry into heaven for the righteous. Those concepts come from cultural cross-pollination with ancient pagan ideas and from misapplication of Scripture. Rather, from death (compared in Scripture to sleep) both the saved and unsaved will live again as respective groups at specific points in time.

But how do we explain those "occurrences"? Today an epidemic of supernatural events saturates our world. Deceased acquaintances seem to materialize out of a fog, appearing to the living; psychics get what they term messages from beyond, the accuracy often astonishing their clients; multitudes seek information on the future; presidents (or their wives?) consult the stars before making decisions on matters of state; UFO lore goes mainstream. One can hardly pick up a magazine or newspaper or turn on the radio or television today without gratuitous exposure to this phenomenon. Sex, violence and the supernatural sell! So don't expect your favorite TV show to do your homework for you.

Deceived At World's End

Scripture is clear that it is possible to handle the word of God deceitfully (2 Corinthians 4:2). When differences of opinion take place within Christendom, both views can be incorrect, but both cannot be correct. These differences can be honest. They can also be dishonest and, even, deceitful. Be assured, with an eternity at stake, wisdom checks out the matter for itself. How can we know if we are deceived?

Many remember an old television quiz show titled "To Tell the Truth." Three contestants answered the questions of the celebrity panel. Only one was telling the truth. The other contestants could say anything they pleased. At the end of the segment, the host asked the question, "Will the real (whoever) please stand up?" After some fidgeting and false starts, one of the three contestants stood up. He or she was telling the truth.

In like manner, let me ask this question: If you are deceived, please stand up.

An increasing number of Christians believe we are living in earth's last days. In recent years I have fallen into conversation on this subject with a number of them of various backgrounds; therefore, anecdotal data tells me few of them would challenge the belief that Christ's second advent is near. Deceptions have existed throughout history, but at no time will the danger be greater than now, at the end of time, just before Christ's return. Scripture has much to say about this:

When the disciples asked how they might know when His coming was near, Jesus said, "Take heed that no one *deceives* you." "Many will come in My name, saying, 'I am the Christ,' and will *deceive* many." "False prophets will rise up and *deceive* many. . . . False christs and false prophets will arise and show great signs and wonders, so as to *deceive*, if possible, even the elect" (Matthew 24: 4,5, 11, 24; Mark 13:5,6).

Notice in particular the phrase "show great signs and wonders." *The deceptions of the last days will be characterized by them.*

Second Thessalonians 2:1-12 is a key Biblical description of the antichrist. Notice verses 3, 9, 10 and 11 in particular.

> Let no one *deceive* you by any means (v. 3); . . . the working of Satan, with all power, signs, and lying wonders, and with all unrighteous *deception* (vss. 9, 10); God will send [permit] them strong *delusion*, that they should believe the lie (v. 11).

These verses depict the strength of *deception* in earth's last days. They harmonize with information from the book of Revelation, the Biblical book of the end. Satan, the power behind and working through antichrist, will deceive *the whole world* (12:9); he will deceive *everyone,* except those whose names are written in God's book of life (13:8, 14). Picture it! Will the majority opinion be trustworthy then?

Interestingly, that deception is even identified as coming through "sorcery," or as the dictionary defines it, the use of "an evil supernatural power over people and their affairs" (18:23).[35] Could Satan deceive the majority into believing the "evil" power is benign? Think about it.

Revelation 19:20 tells how antichrist and his cohorts deceive those who receive the evil "mark of the beast." They deceive by the use of "signs." Although we have no further clues in this text as to the nature of these

---

[35] *Webster's New World Dictionary of the American Language.* (The World Publishing Company: Cleveland and New York, 1966), p. 1391

"signs," adding the information together suggests they are of supernatural origin. Revelation 16:13, symbolizing the powers of antichrist as a dragon, a beast and a false prophet, depicts the signs and miracles of earth's last days as *the work of demons.*

Revelation 20: 3, 8, and 10 describes the fate of Satan for his work of deceiving "the nations," —not a few misguided souls here and there—the nations!

Therefore, let me repeat the question: Will those who are deceived please stand up? Foolish question! It is characteristic of the deceived that they know it not. Who would stand at such a question? No one. But in view of the Biblical picture that *the majority will be deceived in earth's last days, that they will be deceived by "sorcery" and "great signs and wonders," and that those miracles are the work of demons,* perhaps some who might not stand at such a question, might at least pause to wonder.

Heaven Warns Israel

Scripture says God doesn't change; He is the same "yesterday, today and forever" (Malachi 3:6; Hebrews 13:8). Just as God doesn't change, truth doesn't change. Different ages may see a change in emphasis or an advance in previously known truth. But God's character embodies truth—absolute, eternal, and saving. As neither God nor truth change, we may expect that His warnings and admonitions to ancient Israel contain valuable information for us today.

During the time Israel tarried at Sinai, they received from God not only the moral law of ten commandments, but additional regulations as well, covering both the spiritual and civil life of the people. Prominently expressed through these statutes was concern over the matter of sorcery, divination and witchcraft. It is interesting to review some of the statements of Scripture regarding these activities.

- You shall not permit a sorceress [witch] to live (Exodus 22:18).

- Give no regard to mediums and familiar spirits; do not seek after them, to be defiled by them; I am the Lord your God. . . . And the person who turns after mediums and familiar spirits, to prostitute himself with them, I will set My face against that person and cut him off from his people (Leviticus 19:31; 20:6).

- There shall not be found among you anyone who makes his son or daughter pass through the fire,[36] or one who practices witchcraft ["divination," KJV], or a sooth-sayer, or one who interprets omens, or a sorcerer, or one who conjures spells, or a

---

[36] A common practice among Israel's pagan neighbors at the time.

medium, or a spiritist, or one who calls up the dead. For all who do these things are an abomination to the Lord (Deuteronomy 18:10-12).

If these activities were an abomination to the Lord back then, what would He say about the spiritualistic epidemic gripping our world today? Reading horoscopes, consulting tarot cards, calling psychic hot lines seem innocent and harmless. But there is a clear issue of spiritual authority embodied in these activities. These endeavors, so clearly not of God, invite demon forces into the life, and once in, they are not so easily removed. Individuals who have tampered with "the devil's toys," opening up their lives to evil forces, should repudiate these experiences "in the name of Jesus Christ" and go there no more. Continuing such activities invites progressively darker events, which may eventually cause the human to lose control over his or her own life.

If God didn't like it back then, it seems reasonable that He doesn't approve of these activities today. *Someone* is promoting these happenings. If it isn't God, it must be someone else. The experiences are real. Something is happening out there. If the dead are sleeping in their graves, if God has nothing to do with today's spiritualist epidemic, then perhaps the Biblical story of a fallen angel named Satan is true. God's warnings are given for our protection and blessing.

Why It Matters

To the overwhelming abundance of these sensory experiences saturating the media today, the conditionalist says, No. Death is a mere sleep, both to the righteous and to the lost. One falls asleep in death, the next moment—resurrection, like the dawn of a new day. Thus the apostle Paul could say he had a "desire to depart, and to be with Christ" (Philippians 1:23), because no sense of time's passing exists in the tomb. It makes no difference to the dead whether they experience immediate entrance into the presence of God or await the resurrection. It is all the same to them. But is it a question essential to human salvation? After all, many saintly people, whom no one thinks to be lost, have gone to their graves believing in natural immortality (as well as in conditional immortality). Why belabor the question now?

There are several reasons why God would today have us understand the truth of the human condition in death:

1.   Natural immortality, as Christianity presents it, requires the existence of an eternally burning place of torment for the lost. This idea, if true, says either: a) God has no power to put out the fire, thus He is not omnipotent, or b) it burns through His decree, which raises questions regarding His loving character. Therefore, our understanding of death reflects our understanding of God.

2.   Natural immortality makes plausible the infinite number of sensory experiences many are having that seem to indicate "the dead know" *something* and continue to interact with the living. Conditional immortality views these events as Satanic deceptions. If *human* magicians can perform feats that baffle our minds, if *human* actors can portray historical figures so accurately they appear to be channeling their subject, what can *demons* do? As invisible witnesses to our lives, would they not know everything they needed to know to execute a believable impersonation of our deceased loved ones? These experiences position themselves against the great weight of Biblical evidence that says the sleeping dead "know not anything."

3.   It affords opportunity for students of Scripture to say whom they believe to be the "liar" in the Eden scenario, God or Satan.

4.   Truth builds on truth; it cannot build on error. It is impossible to see a nondestructive God in Scripture, except through the eyes of *conditional* immortality, which holds that humans are already dead in trespasses and sins. Therefore, in conditional immortality the energy of God need not be expended to remove life from humans; rather, it must be generated to keep them alive. Again for emphasis: God expends His energy to generate and maintain life. Any time He ceases to support the life of plant, animal or human, that life ceases to exist, as did the pretentious fig tree that Jesus cursed. Without God's presence, good will and life-giving energy, there is no life—human or otherwise. The view of God as a nondestructive Being is the next natural unfolding of the doctrine of *conditional* immortality.

John Three Sixteen

We repeat the familiar words of John 3:16 without really catching the meaning. "For God so loved the world that He gave His only begotten Son that whosoever believeth in Him should not *perish* but have everlasting life." Here again God presents the contrast between our choices inside and outside Himself. What does it mean to "perish"? We have not understood how thoroughly dead we are in trespasses and sins. The enemy has had a field day convincing us otherwise, but Scripture is clear: We have no life outside the hope Jesus brought to the human race in Himself.

Where Did Jesus Go When He Died?

The Scriptural description of death as "sleep" illuminates the cross, just as the cross illuminates our understanding of the fate of the lost. We cannot leave this subject without delving more deeply into what it meant to Jesus to die the sinner's death. Christ's death is often described as the most terrible ever experienced upon this planet. But in what respect was it so? While He endured great physical torture, others have died in pain, perhaps even more physically painful deaths than His. In what respect was His death different and far more terrible? Insights from conditional immortality help answer these questions.

When He cried, "It is finished. Father, into Your hands I commend My spirit" (Luke 23:46; John 19:30), the words were heavy with meaning.

As Jesus hung on the cross that day, the sins of a guilty world fastened upon Him, *separating Him from the Father*, His one strength and solace in life. Strong emotions horrified Him with the thought that He was saying goodbye to life *forever*, since that is the sinner's destiny apart from God. Surely Satan, his own fate hanging in the balance, tormented Him with the thought that if He allowed Himself to surrender to death, for Him there would be no awaking. With this great weight of darkness upon Him, our Savior spoke the words of surrender to the will of the Father, releasing into His hand the right to do as He would with the life of His only-begotten Son.

Where did Jesus go when He died? If He, as the Sin-bearer, went to an ever-burning place of eternal torment, I challenge any Bible scholar to show this from the word of God. It isn't there. If He, as the righteous Son of the living God, resorted to the throne of His heavenly Father, Scripture doesn't mention it. On the contrary. After His resurrection He said to Mary, "Do not cling to Me; for I have not yet ascended to my Father" (John 20:17). Scripture doesn't say that Christ went anywhere.

The great weight of Biblical evidence says He went to sleep—forever, if that's what His Father chose for Him. Gethsemane, where He sweat great drops of blood in anticipation of the struggle before Him, demonstrates the reality of His torment. He felt the mental anguish the lost will feel, when they at last see what they have lost and face their own hopeless condition. Yes, He arose from the grave, an outcome left entirely in His Father's hands,[37] but He Himself *could not see through the portal of the tomb*. Why did He do it? Because there was no other means whereby humans could escape eternal nonexistence. Christ took upon Himself the justice of the universe toward sinners, and we received the mercy.

There are no flaws in the character of God. There are no inconsistencies. He is love. Everything else about His character rests on that foundation.

---

[37]Jesus died as the Sin-bearer. Justice allowed God the Father to resurrect Him based upon Christ's sinless human life. However, Christ had no assurance of a resurrection when He surrendered to the grave. When He cried, "Father, into Your hands I commend My spirit," these were words of true release and acceptance of whatever the Father's will for Him might be.

APPENDIX C

Conditional Immortality
and Final Punishment

Do humans have inherent life that cannot die ("natural immortality")? Is death merely a transition to eternal reward or punishment? Or is life inherent only in God, who grants eternal life on certain conditions ("conditional immortality")? The former, the traditional view, is accepted by the great majority of humans—Christians and others. The latter, although the minority view, has been held by some throughout time.

Since the thesis of *Light On the Dark Side of God* relies on the minority view, it seemed necessary to give that view additional exposure. However, the need to limit my topic to a defense of the nondestructive nature of God did not permit as thorough an exploration of the nature of death as the situation called for.

Thus I was pleased to find others have supplied the necessary support for the concept of *conditional* human immortality. Following is information regarding several of these works.

Daring To Differ: Adventures in Conditional Immortality, by Sidney Hatch, Th.M.[38]

The author takes a controversial Bible subject and, without recourse to theological jargon, manages to make it clear and accessible to the average reader. Here are some quotations from the book jacket and preface of this very readable book:

---

[38]See footnote 34, page 106.

We are all of us indebted to responsible scholars of the Bible who dare to question cherished tradition. These are the Christian trailblazers who urge us to throw off the shackles of uncritical submission to "what we have always believed."

A distinguished example . . . is Pastor Sidney Hatch. His daring exploration into the question of Conditional Immortality . . . is loaded with dynamite. . Pastor Hatch's style of writing makes the theological content of his message accessible even to the inexperienced readers of theology.

—Sir Anthony Buzzard
From the Foreword to
Daring To Differ

This book is about conditional immortality. If the term is new to you or sounds strange, please don't let it scare you away. I'll explain it in a moment. I only ask for open minds, willing to hear what I have to say. . . .

Accepting the concept of conditional immortality has been a liberating experience for me. It has transformed my religious faith, my life, and my ministry. It can do the same for you. It may come as a relief for many, and a surprise for some, to realize that God is a kind and fair God.

—From Preface To
Daring To Differ

I pointed out that 'the breath of life' was not an immortal soul but simply the life force, something possessed by all living things. It was then that the man to my right, with his great booming voice, called out, "Wait a minute, wait a minute!"

I realized that day, as never before, the impact of Genesis 2:7. There are many people in this world who possess an almost fanatical loyalty to the Greek doctrine of the immortality of the soul. It matters not that neither the term nor the concept are found in Scripture; it is still the foundation of their religion.

There is a certain analogy between my experience . . . and Paul's experience two thousand years ago in Athens. The Athenians listened to him until he mentioned the resurrection of the dead. Then, we read, "some mocked: and others said, We will hear thee again of this matter."

The Athenians believed in the immortality of the soul. Luke's account in the Book of Acts indicates that, to them, resurrection from the dead was ridiculous.

The doctrines of conditional immortality have a way of breaking up meetings—if one dares to preach them.

—Sidney Hatch, Th.M.
Daring To Differ: Adventures
In Conditional Immortality (p. 7)

The Fire That Consumes, by Edward William Fudge[39]

I requested and received permission to reproduce material from the book jacket of *The Fire That Consumes* by Edward William Fudge, an evangelical theologian, to show that the author's purpose was not to defend his personal orthodoxy. On the contrary, his findings, after exhaustive research were the opposite of what he expected them to be.

His Chapter 12 deserves special attention, as it shows that, from a conditionalist perspective, there was far, far more to Calvary than a cross.

The following book jacket information accurately describes *The Fire That Consumes*:

> *The Fire That Consumes*, by Edward William Fudge, is a provocative biblical and historical study of the controversial doctrine of final punishment. The book recommends itself by its careful and thorough research. Fudge investigates both Old and New Testaments on the doctrine of final punishment—but does not stop there. He also examines the Jewish writings between the Testaments as well as relevant material from the Apostolic Fathers down to the present.
>
> Like a tireless detective searching out every clue, Fudge employs biblical exegesis, systematic theology and a critical eye as he delves into a much-neglected subject. No assumptions are left unchallenged—including the author's own—and several are called into serious question. Writes Fudge:
>
> "This study has elicited a spectrum of emotions in the author—despair and relief, anxiety and peace, incredulity and final surrender. The position presented must stand or fall on the evidence, and that evidence is not personal desire, human philosophy or ecclesiastical tradition but the living and abiding, infallible Word of God."
>
> Publisher
> Providential Press

> While the subject of this study by Mr. Fudge is one on which there is no unanimity among evangelical Christians, it is at the same time one on which they have often engaged in fierce polemic with one another. . . . What is called for, rather, is the fellowship of patient Bible study. It is the fruit of such study that Mr. Fudge presents here. . . .
>
> It gives me great pleasure to commend Mr. Fudge's exposition of this subject. All that he has to say is worthy of careful consideration, but there is special value in those chapters where he examines the testimony of successive sections of the Holy Scriptures.
>
> F. F. Bruce, The University
> of Manchester, England

---

[39]Church of Christ theologian. Houston: Providential Press, 1982.

The doctrine of hell and the final judgment of the wicked is much neglected in the modern church. Edward Fudge attributes this in part to the traditional understanding of hell as eternal conscious torment. In a thorough reexamination of the biblical data on this subject, the author concludes that God intends to destroy the wicked rather than make them suffer forever. In this extensive and effective book, Mr. Fudge seriously challenges the popular assumption, more Greek than scriptural, that God plans to raise the wicked to immortality in order to inflict upon them everlasting pain. I hope this book will rekindle interest in an important biblical theme which should not be neglected. I know of no book which answers Mr. Fudge's powerful case for conditional immortality.

Clark H. Pinnock
McMaster Divinity College
Canada

Why has eternal conscious punishment so long been assumed the clear teaching of Scripture? In this thorough and convincing exposition, Edward Fudge proposes that conditional immortality is a just and biblically supportable alternative to the view that God would allow His creation to suffer unspeakable, endless conscious torment in hell. He carefully and cogently argues that the unbeliever will be finally destroyed, and simply cease to exist. For those who wish to understand the conditionalist argument on final punishment, even if they are not among those who seriously entertain the possibility, this book will be found indispensable.

Leonard George Goss
Editorial Director
Evangelical Book Club, USA

I hope Mr. Fudge's book will be read far and wide. Its subject is of great importance to every Christian. Our view of the afterlife affects our view of God and deserves much thought and study.

The author aims to be biblical, reverent and fair, and in this he succeeds admirably, showing soundness and independence of judgment. He is also lucid and easy to read. He makes his main points with force and persuasiveness.

John W. Wenham
Pastor and InterVarsity
Author, Oxford, England

The Mystery of Salvation, by The Doctrine Commission of the Church of England[40]

In 1995 the aforesaid Doctrine Commission of the Church of England took the courageous step of publishing this report, which clearly supports concepts of conditional immortality. The report (actually a small book) carries this preface:

> This Report, like its two predecessors, is published under the authority of the House of Bishops and is commended by the House to the Church for study.
>
> On behalf of the House of Bishops
> —George Cantuar, Chairman

It further includes the following quotations:

> The hope of the righteous, of the people of God, is resurrection. The wicked also will be raised to judgement. The Day of the Lord, the day of messianic hope, is the day of resurrection. The predominant theme of first Jewish and then Christian hope in the face of death is that of the resurrection of the body (p. 190).

> The soul is "'the information-bearing pattern' of the body . . ." held in God's mind (p. 191).

> In the past the imagery of hell-fire and eternal torment and punishment, often sadistically expressed, has been used to frighten men and women into believing. Christians have professed appalling theologies which made God into a sadistic monster and left searing psychological scars on many (p. 199).

Final Note: Please keep in mind that the works mentioned in this Appendix *do not* support the view that God is a nonparticipant in the destruction of the lost, as does *Light On the Dark Side of God.* These authors do, however, support the idea that life is a gift to us from the cross of Jesus Christ, not something we inherently possess—a position critical to the thesis of the present work.

---

[40]Available from Church House Bookshop, 31 Great Smith Street, London SWIP 3BN England, $18.11 US, including s/h by Visa/Mastercard. E-mail: Info@chp.u-net.com.

Other Available Titles

The Two Covenants.   The message of righteousness by faith in a simplified, question and answer form, based on the writings of A. T. Jones and E. J. Waggoner.

The Power of God's Word. Reveals the dynamics by which the gospel activates in the life of the believer.

The Hour of His Judgment Is Come. The Biblical picture of the judgment in its various phases; i.e., the judgment of the dead, the judgment of the living, final judgment. Why a judgment? Also contains related information.

Absolute Rest. Much good information about God's character and personality and what it means to the Christian to rest *in Him.*

The Lord's Day of Rest. A pamphlet giving a Biblical look at the Christian Sabbath.

Is the Human Soul Immortal?   This pamphlet takes the reader through Scripture to learn what it says about death.

Many more available titles.

Contact :

Truth For the Final Generation
P. O. Box 216
Caldwell, Idaho 83605

www.OIGC.net
www.TruthInJesus.org
Info@TruthInJesus.org